if i gave you

God's

phone number....

if i gave you

God's

phone number....

Searching for Spirituality
in America

MARE CROMWELL

to jenna:
— sister spiritual source
❦ beautiful wisdom and
compassion. ☺

❦ *[signature]* 9/11

PAMOON
PRESS

Published by Pamoon Press,
an imprint of Sacred Dog Productions LLC.

Grateful acknowledgment is made to the following for permission to reprint
previously published material:
HarperCollins Publishers Inc: text from A RETURN TO LOVE by Marianne
Williamson. Copyright © 1992 by Marianne Williamson. Reprinted by
permission of HarperCollins Publishers. *Merton Legacy Trust:* quote from a talk
given by Thomas Merton in August, 1965 and published in Cistercian Studies in
1970 as "A Life Free From Care." Copyright @ 1970 by Thomas Merton.
Reprinted by permission of Merton Legacy Trust. *Anna Pool:* excerpt from song
"Be Still and Know" recorded on *Oh Free Spirit* by Anna Pool, Be Light Music.
Copyright © 1993 by Anna Pool. Reprinted by permission of Anna Pool.

ISBN 0-9717032-0-5

Library of Congress Control Number 2002091373

Designed by Toni D. Jones/Brainstorm Studios
John Walker/Lazarus Designs
Cover Photograph by Pat Powers and Cherryl Schafer, Photodisc

Pamoon Press
P.O. Box 5381
Baltimore, Maryland 21209
www.pamoonpress.com

Printed in the United States of America

10 9 8 7 6 5 4 3 2 1

First Edition

Dedicated to

Jasmine, a sublime teacher of spirit and life
and to the spirit of Bill Stapp, which lives on in so many of us
who were graced by his compassionate, visionary ways.

ACKNOWLEDGMENTS

Writing a book about God is a daunting process. I could not have done this without the help, in a myriad of ways, from many, many people.

First, the foundation of this book are all those who invited me into their homes and their spiritual lives so that I could interview them. You answered my questions with a courage and openness that amazed me. You are the book and the work that follows it. Thank you barely suffices in expressing my gratitude to you.

I would also like to express my deep appreciation to everyone who read all or parts of book drafts and gave me guidance on how to improve it. If I have forgotten your name, please forgive me. This book had so many incarnations that some of you may have slipped through the cracks. Know that I am deeply grateful regardless. Thank you to Barbara Thompson, John Alexander, Buff Conklin, Ed Scheminger, Jim Farnham, Jason Cohen, Randy Whitlock, Marwin Smith, Randy Shay, Tina Borden, Marcia Wiley, Ruthie Cromwell, Franklyn Rodgers and Sarah Lord for all of your wonderful, creative thoughts. In addition, my community's writing club was a gift of timely constructive criticism that set the book solidly on its final course.

And then there are the transcribers who helped me keep my sanity by doing some of the nitty-est, gritty-est work in the whole process, in particular Jenny Goldberg, Mark Montgomery and Elaine Lewis. You all are excellent.

There are a few people who took on significant roles as the book reached its final stages of completion. Sarabelle Walker not only read various parts of the book several times but was available for grammatical direction over the phone at all hours of the day and night. Jim Cole of the Writer's Doubt Club, now the Writer's Published Club, was great support (and remember, Jim, I pay for dinners after the book is published!). Mark Luce was invaluable for his creative inspiration and photographic spontaneity.

Christopher Noël is a very gentle, compassionate editor who pushed me to "go deeper" and did so in a way that made me appreciate his editorial skills even more. I mean, you're not supposed to like your editor. But Chris, you have mastered a way to encourage the writer's light to shine even brighter. I bow to your skills. Juliette Hayes came along to help me cross every *t* and dot every *i*. And then went on to share her beautiful spiritual revelations. Philip and Tracy Iglehart, I hope your garden glows as much as I know my websites will. Thanks for being willing to exchange.

John Walker stepped in to keep the ship afloat and on course as the book designer. I sincerely hope you have caught up on your sleep since, John. Your design work is fabulous.

Kwame Alexander is a poet, writer, playwright and he also happens to be this book's "Book Guardian." As a consultant, Kwame, you held my hand through thick and thin so that others can now hold this book in their hands. Let's keep the adventure rolling.

For all of her unconditional support and almost daily phone calls in the final months of writing that kept me buoyed in the despair of my "dark" writing cave, Sandi Athey's love and support was incredible.

Tom Speers, I am honored to call you family and neighbor. You directed me to find the Bible on the web, and a deeper understanding of your path and heart in our conversations. If every church/mosque/synagogue/temple was led by such a person as compassionate and humble as you, surely our world would be closer to God.

Also a deep thank you to my parents for bringing me into this Earthwalk, so that I could be such a student of spirit.

To my housemates, Max and Suzanne, two of the finest feline friends/entertainers a writer could have, you're the best.

And D. You know who you are. "Thank you" barely touches how you have helped me.

And ultimately, to the Creator/God and all your manifestations...Wow. This life is an adventure I have come to learn to celebrate. My humble gratitude is a drop in the sea of love and joy You are.

Contents

Introduction

I have wanted to talk to God for as long as I can remember. As a young child in the Catholic Church, I was taught that prayer was the same as talking to God. But when I prayed, I wanted to hear God's responses back to me. I wanted Him to answer my questions. But I never got a response back. As I got older and drifted away from the Catholic Church, I was not sure who God was at all. Was the Creator a He, She or It? My need for answers grew even greater.

This book has surfaced as a part of my seeking. The idea came to me during a very difficult time in my mid-thirties. I was not sure where I was going or what I was doing, or even who I was. My confusion about God was just as great. I longed for answers and clarity. It struck me that if I was confused about God, perhaps I could glean some wisdom from other people's thoughts on this great mystery.

I had left a demanding job running an environmental nonprofit in 1994 and chose to not take a full-time job at the time so I could slow down. I had been on and off antidepressants for several years and felt like one of the walking wounded. My priority was to try to heal the pervasive inner pain that had haunted me for years. I thought that by slowing down, I could better focus on making my inner world whole.

I moved back to Baltimore, my hometown, and stored most of my belongings to minimize expenses. I was starting life over again. A local plant nursery offered me part-time work and in time I found some gardening clients who hired me to take care of their flowerbeds. But more than anything, I created the time and space to walk and think and feel.

Shortly after returning to Baltimore, I moved in with a seventy-eight-year-old widow in the countryside north of the city. Judith's husband had died the year before and I was her first boarder. She led a quiet life and was a devout Episcopalian. For hours Judith and I would talk about God, prayer, meditation, and spiritual ways to live. Every week she invited me to attend church with her but I resisted. There was something about the confinement of a church that I was not comfortable with. Instead, I would walk the rolling fields and forests around her country home and try to find God/peace there. One morning just before she left for church, I joked with her about being able to call God on the phone. "Wouldn't it be a fascinating question to ask other people?" I asked her. That was in the summer of 1995.

Spirituality Shopping

By the time I met Judith, I had been a serious spirituality shopper for a number of years. Brought up as the middle child of seven children in a rather unhappy Catholic family, I received an intense indoctrination in Catholicism in my early years. Although we did not attend Catholic school, we woke up very early for Mass on all holy days and church on Sunday was obligatory.

When I was a young child, our family had an evening ritual of prayer before bed. Kneeling in front of the couch in a little line, my older brothers and I would pray for the conversion of Russia and other assorted Catholic petitions ~ many of which made no sense to my three- or four-year-old understanding of the world. I have early recollections of rebelling against the prayer session (it hurt to kneel on the carpet) and being strictly punished for it.

I did take my prayers seriously, though. My parents

dropped the kneeling routine once more children were born but I used to pray alone at night in my bed on a regular basis anyway. I intensely pleaded with God to allow me to become a saint. According to what we had learned in Sunday School, being a saint was the ultimate goal. My image of God was that He did hear us but He was very busy. He actually had the entire Universe in an aquarium on a sunny window sill in His den. There was far more to His house than the den but that is where we, along with all the other galaxies and solar systems and planets, were kept. Needless to say, my concept of God has changed since I was a small girl.

I do remember enjoying the folk Masses at our Catholic parish in the '70s. But those were the only times I felt any joy in church. Beyond that, the services were very serious and boring. The pews were never comfortable to sit on and the rituals seemed empty. When I left home for college, I sampled the small Catholic Church there and decided that I had more meaningful things to do which did not include any church. I opted to sleep in or go for long walks in the rolling land beyond the college campus.

After college when I was in my mid-twenties, I got involved with a serious boyfriend who opened me up emotionally as no man had done before. Jim gave me such nurturing and supportive love, it filled a large void in me hungry for such positive attention. His constant kind words and affirmation of me lifted me out of the melancholiness that I lapsed into so easily. It was the first time in my life that I felt a glimpse of what "love" really could be. The relationship lasted only ten months as we got to know each other and realized that our life paths were taking us in very different directions. When it ended I collapsed into a deep spiritual crisis. Our breakup exposed a gaping spiritual hole inside me ~ a pit that had always been there but had never really been touched before.

That familiar pit dated back to my young childhood. I

was always one of the "weird" kids. There were the popular cute girls at the center of all social activities and then there were the few of us ousted to the periphery. Either our clothes were odd or we just didn't have the social skills to make it in the social circles. I fitted in the latter group. I did not invite classmates home very often and was alone much of the time.

It was all that I could do to get my parents' singular attention. So I was sick a great deal; this included being diagnosed with pneumonia three times by age thirteen. More than anything I relished getting all the attention at home with my mother. The house was peaceful, I could read to my heart's content and she would dote on me with ginger ale and crackers.

But I grew up feeling as if there was some fatal flaw in me. Why wasn't I as popular or my grades as good as some of the other girls? I knew I wasn't stupid. But I never felt like I was meant for school. As childhood shifted into adolescence the experience of being odd only heightened. Sadness and insecurities were ongoing emotions in my high school years. The dominant voice in my head that echoed incessantly was: "I am not good enough." If it wasn't a mean classmate that told me that indirectly, it was one of my four brothers who teased me mercilessly about the kinds of things that older brothers love to torture sisters about: my looks, my weight or any other sensitive topic. The exact words are not important. What is important was that my self-esteem was quite tattered by the time I left home for college. I had no concept what it felt like to be confident or love myself. I only knew the inner voices that held me prisoner to a negative self-image.

Years later I picked up an article about depression in children and read about the behaviors that such children exhibit. As I scanned down the list, I was stunned. I recognized myself in the article all too clearly. I did not like to be touched or held. I kept to myself as much as possible.

I had few friends and hated getting out of bed for school. There was little joy in me. My parents could never have seen it since they were so wrapped up in their own struggles, so I numbly lived out deep inner sadness and confusion outside of their realm of awareness. I was never at the point of being suicidal but I did walk around in a gray murky despair much of the time.

College was a mixed experience where I was grateful to be out of high school but my emotions gyrated semester to semester. During my freshman year, a guy I was very attracted to callously ended a brief fling and I was so devastated that I ended up in the hospital with pneumonia ~ again. I remember focusing all of my energy into my classes for the rest of the semester and ignoring any other romantic possibilities. The rest of my college career was checkered with deep introverted academic time, some good moments with close friends and few forays into romantic liaisons. Near the end of my senior year, one of my friends confided in me that she loved me as a friend, but she never understood me. This only further cemented my sense that I was a flawed being.

Most of my life I felt as if I was spinning out of control. I have since come to realize that I am one of those people born sensitive ~ born to reverberate with any and all emotional chords echoing around me. The more strident the emotion, the more my body quivers. If someone is arguing near me, my whole body takes it in like a dry sponge absorbs turbulent water. I literally shake with the depth of emotion and it becomes absorbed into my system, sometimes taking years to dissipate.

So when Jim and I broke up when I was twenty-five, and his love for me disappeared, I was devastated. I realized that I had not been able to truly love him for I had such emptiness and fear inside. The pain that surfaced from our pulling away from each other rose like a huge bubble to choke me. It was excruciating. When he was gone, I could barely get out of bed in the morning to live my day. I lapsed into the familiar wallow of self-hate and spiritual emptiness that I had known for much of my life already.

Hungry for answers, wisdom, love and any semblance of inner peace, I became an intense seeker. The first thing I sought out was a career counselor since I was so confused about my life work then. After several sessions discussing my interests, he recommended that I consider seeing him as a regular therapy client because of the emotional issues that I was grappling with. He told me one day: "You are the type of person who needs a lot of love." This only further validated to me that I was intrinsically flawed. Was I born with a gap in the love quotient that most people don't have? And after a few more sessions, he recommended that I consider antidepressants. I refused.

I knew that part of my inner pain was a spiritual void. Around that same time I had started taking yoga classes and learned of a very large center in New England called Kripalu that offered programs in self-growth and yoga. After another brief relationship crashed a year after Jim and I broke up, I escaped in desperation to this center for a weekend program. The insecurity and anxiety in my life was becoming unbearable.

Kripalu was an ashram and holistic center led by a guru. It offered dozens of programs for guests based on the guru's teachings. As soon as I walked in and saw the warmth on the staff's faces, I felt a grace that touched my core. From when I was twenty-five to thirty-six, Kripalu became the filling station for my spirit, much to the chagrin of my very Catholic father. Through the teachings of the guru, I started to learn ways to forgive and love myself and experience what a spiritual community is about.

Professionally, I continued to pursue my environmental work ~ as a workaholic. I enrolled in graduate school at the University of Michigan, completed a master's in natural science and immediately was hired by my professor to coordinate an international project. The hours were exhausting and the ongoing stress of funding and administrative challenges sapped me. I would put all my energy into work and had little left for any relationship exploration. I dated a few men but felt safer being alone at the end of the evening. Wrung out and exhausted spiritually, I would return to the yoga center once or twice a year to fill up and then head back out to "prove myself." I even went to India to experience yoga on a deeper level and became a disciple of the guru there.

What I learned at Kripalu did bring me temporary glimpses of peace. But my emptiness still gnawed away inside. Whatever I learned at the center was not strong enough to stave off my inner emotional pain. The yoga retreats were mere Band-Aids on a gaping psychic gash. I also continued psychotherapy but it, too, barely soothed the agony. Eventually I surrendered to antidepressants just to be able to continue working.

About the same time that I quit my job to slow down in 1994, the guru admitted to sexual scandals and was forced to leave the center. I was already feeling rather lost having just left my job and the security it provided me, and this only made me feel worse. It felt like my spiritual refuge had just vaporized. I didn't know where to turn for a sense of spiritual security but I was still determined to find that peace. I continued to slow down and search.

So I went spirituality shopping again. Moving back to Baltimore, I tried to meditate with a Zen group but their strict approach did not suit me. I even tried another Hindu group but the guru overtones of their spiritual leader felt too familiar to Kripalu and hence repelled me. The Unitarian Church appealed to me along with the Quakers but they still did not feel right. The Unitarian Church did not have enough spiritual substance to their sermons and I sought more teaching than the Quakers offered, much as I respected the inner wisdom they promoted. Both churches were committed to social activism, which I thought was wonderful. However, something I could not quite identify still felt lacking to me.

I even thought about trying the Catholic Church again. I went back to my childhood church alone on Christmas Eve to join in the Christmas carols and experience the Mass again. However, ten minutes into the service, I realized that the only people who were supposed to sing were the choir and several operatic cantors. When the priest started talking about begging God for His mercy, I had had enough. I had learned enough by that time to know that I already had God's mercy and love. I did not need to beg for it and feel lacking in it as the Catholic Church wanted me to believe. This was one message that Kripalu had instilled in me.

I kept searching. I knew there were answers out there and healing that I just had not found yet. Determined to find that peace, I continued to seek out psychotherapy, spiritual teachers and healers. Everyone I spoke with pushed and prodded me to go deeper and be open.

The Process

Once I realized that asking people about calling God up might not be just a joke but a serious proposition, I bought a tape recorder. At first I asked anyone I met. Judith's friends who came over to visit were a captive audience.

Gradually I became more comfortable asking anyone: the man in the workshop, the daughter of the caretaker, the guy at the sweatlodge and on and on. I wanted to find people from as many walks of life and religious beliefs as I could. In time, I actively sought people from outside my circle of connections and venues to broaden the scope. Friends or contacts helped by introducing me to people they knew. The most challenging interview to set up was with a man on death row. It was only because of a newspaper article on men under the death penalty locally that I found the name of a prisoner to contact.

I would always have an initial conversation with those who were referred to me. Some I interviewed. Others I didn't. Generally I would ask the person if they were interested only after we had spoken a bit and they appeared to be open to sharing. My decisions were based on a purely instinctual feeling as to whether they might be a good interview prospect. Even then I never knew what they would say.

I tried to interview people at their homes to get a better sense of them. At times this was not possible and then we conducted the interview where I lived. Regardless of location, I would encourage these people to talk about their lives in order to provide some background.

There were several people I very much wanted to talk with but they refused, for reasons I'll never truly know. One was a forty-one-year-old woman dying of cancer and, perhaps, my question was too intrusive as she grappled with her own innumerable questions about death and God's role in it.

In some ways, my interviews were akin to being a voyeur with permission. At first I felt like a lonely, lost person walking outside in the cold seeking a glimpse of the inside of someone else's warm spiritual sanctuary. My glimpse was the interview. I could never be in their inner sanctum but perhaps I could learn something from them to create my own sanctuary. As the book evolved, so I evolved. My need to be a voyeur grew less as I found insights from both the interviews and other experiences to help me create my own sanctum.

Toward the end of the seven years of interviewing, I was more curious than spiritually needy. My sense of God and spirit was more clear because of what I had learned from various teachers I had found during this period. But I still conducted more interviews to explore a broader representation of the beliefs in our American culture. People lead such different lives and have such fascinating perspectives, I just wanted to hear their thoughts.

The Interview

I would tell each interviewee in advance that the interview started with the question: "If I gave you God's phone number, what would you do with it?" And then the interview led from there. This always made them pause. Usually they would launch into an immediate response to the question. I would have to cut them off so they would not have to repeat themselves later when we did the formal interview on tape.

I had to assure some that, for the sake of the interview, they could assume that such a number exists and that, yes, God would answer. If they said they would use the number and they had certain questions for God, I would turn their questions around and ask them how they think God might respond.

I marveled at how, in the course of the conversation, people would ultimately tell me who their God is ~ if they had one. Yet, I know that if I had directly asked these individuals to tell me about their God at the beginning of the interview, most of them would have been quite reluctant to share. We rarely talk about that very personal part of our spiritual lives. But given the proposition of a phone number, most people gradually felt safe expressing their beliefs to me.

I loved doing the interviews. There were always surprises. Within some an interesting phenomenon took place. When I spoke with those who had embraced a deep spiritual path, our simple act of conversing was transformed into something far more powerful. It felt as if we were being wrapped in a spiritual cocoon of warmth and love. This happened several times. There are times that I have experienced this feeling, either sitting alone in front of my altar at home or after a blissful day of hiking in deep wilderness or during a very heartfelt conversation with a good friend. But in the process of some of the interviews, I felt it much more strongly. I would walk out of those sessions feeling as if I had been transported closer to the spiritual realms.

Those interviews that felt so God-loving brought to mind the Biblical quote: "For when two or three are gathered in my name, there I am in the midst of them." (Matthew 18:20) Listening to those interview tapes and writing them up would transport me again. I know that was one of the reasons that I did the book ~ for those glimpses of spirit and connection.

When I first started the interview process, I told each person that I would not use their names to encourage them to feel uninhibited about sharing any controversial beliefs. As I collected more interviews, though, some people asked that their name be used so I honored them.

I cannot say whether the interviews had any lasting influence on the people I talked with. I know that some had a revelation while we were talking. My questions would sometimes prompt them to find some clarity as they considered their beliefs more deeply. One woman told me afterwards that she was very moved by the discussion and felt closer to God after it. Another person who was an atheist sent me articles that further supported his beliefs after we did the interview. Perhaps many of the interviewees went deeper into their belief systems regardless of what they were.

Each interview offered a snapshot of that person's beliefs in that moment. I imagine if I were to talk with these individuals again, their thoughts would be different since people do change.

Often people would ask me what I would do with God's number, if I had it. I would always tell them that it depended on the day and what issues I was grappling with. I knew that my real goal was to discover the number itself so I could have ongoing conversations. I did not think I would actually find it but only get closer and closer to the potential of it. In truth, my searchings led me to amazing people who offered me powerful insights into how to develop a strong connection with God ~ into learning the number.

This book is a mosaic of spirituality and religion. It offers glimpses of how people with diverse religious/spiritual backgrounds contemplate talking with God and their perceptions of this great mystery, sometimes unique unto themselves. This book is also a window into my spiritual journey. It has been part of my healing process.

With the deepest humility I give this book now to you.

Mare Cromwell
Baltimore
March 2002

Note:
I collected close to fifty interviews over the process of seven years. Those that made the cut were transcribed and then edited to remove the repetitious or not so relevant parts. All grammatical inconsistencies were corrected. Great effort was made to maintain the integrity of each person's voice, however.

CHAPTER 1

GOD'S LITTLE STONES

KATE HARVEY*

AGE: 8

DO NOT DECEIVE YOURSELVES
BY JUST LISTENING TO GOD'S WORD;
INSTEAD, PUT IT INTO PRACTICE.

~ JAMES 1:22

Shortly after I bought my tape recorder, I made a road trip up to New England for an environmental conference. En route I spent two days with some good friends from college who lived in Philadelphia. It was fall, and I remember their upper-middle-class neighborhood bathed in the deep, golden orange and red of expansive trees as I drove up to their house.

My friends had done rather well financially, with Philip as an investment banker and Carole working as an interior designer. Their two children, Kate and Christopher, had the polish of affluent, disciplined children. Both attended private schools. Everything about their house spoke of cultivated taste.

With the new tape recorder burning a hole in my bag, I asked Philip and Carole, after the kids went to bed that first night, whether they might be open to my interviewing Kate

---

*not her real name

and Christopher. They thought it was a fun idea and gave me their blessing. The next day I mentioned it to the kids over breakfast before school, and they were humored by it and said yes. Kate, the younger and more enthusiastic of the two, wanted to go first. So I promised that as soon as she returned from school, we would do it.

Kate was a very bubbly, attractive eight-year-old with long brown hair and bright hazel eyes. As soon as she was home later that afternoon, she dropped her books off in the front hall and announced that she was ready. For the interview, she chose to sit in the family room on the couch next to one of her family's German shepherds. It was challenging for her to stay still while she talked. She squirmed all over the couch and wrestled with the dog.

(Kate and Christopher are Episcopalian. On Sundays, they regularly attend Sunday school while their parents are at the service.)

✦

If I gave you God's phone number, what would you do with it?

I would call Him. I would ask Him how He made the world.

I would dial the number and then: "Drringgg..." God would answer the phone. And I would ask Him, "How did you make the world?"

How do you think God might answer your question?

I'm not sure what God would say back. He may ask me how I think He made the world. I would tell Him that I really think He made the world with His magical powers and His brain. He is very smart.

I also wonder if God might have been very, very lonely, so He might have wanted a better home and some people to live with Him so everybody would make friends. So we would have friendship and that stuff.

That's a wonderful idea. So, do you think that this is a good world that God has made?

Yes, I do think that this is a good world, but we have to work a little harder on it. We need to do things like throw trash in the garbage more and recycle things. And we could make the world a better place by doing what we're supposed to do, like not watch TV all day. That's one of the things that my mom tells me.

Any other questions?

Let's think here. I would then ask God if He was the first person to live. I think He was the first person to live because that is how He made the world.

But how was He born? Did He just poof and become alive? What I think might have happened is that there was this little cloud and POOF ~ He came out of the cloud. But He was about seven or nine or ten. Because if He was a baby, nobody would have been able to take care of Him. And then He made the world and could eat and drink and take care of Himself and have his life.

Then I would ask another question to God: "Will you never, ever, ever die? If you do die, would Jesus take over your place?" I don't know how God would answer that. But I don't think He's going to die.

Actually I don't know who God was born from either because He is God. But if He wasn't God and He was Jesus, I would believe that Jesus was God's son.

Any other thoughts about God?

I think God is a body that is inside of me and He is helping me with my life. And He is also on each side of me and also in you and everybody else in the world, too. Sometimes He has little traps for you that you have to get over. This could be when you get into fights with somebody.

Can you give me an example?

Suppose I was playing a game of cards like Spit, and the other person started yelling at me because he didn't like the card that I put down. This could be a test from God. We have to try not to yell back at that person and get into a huge fight. God wants us to be good and show that we have good sportsmanship.

It's as if God puts these little stones in your way, and you can't get them out of your way unless you try really hard. You have to work it out but it's hard. God tests us to see if we can do it.

God wants to know whether we know to do the right thing. He wants us to be good but not perfect. As good as you can. Don't be like a perfect little angel, every day doing everything perfectly. But every day you want to try to do most things right. This could mean being nice to each other, like in friendship.

So God wants you to be good...

Lots of times I do things and want to ask God if I did the right thing. Like with my brother, Christopher. Christopher always barges into my room and never asks if he can come in. He just comes in and sits on my bed and stays there. I ask him to get out, but he won't go. I always knock on the door before I go into his room. He always says, "No, you cannot come in." Even when my parents say that I can go into his room, he won't let me in. But he just barges into my room. That is just not fair.

So last night I told my dad about this. I would want to ask God about whether I am doing the right thing in telling my father about this.

That's a big question. What do you think God would say back to you?

That is one of the hardest questions. [Pause] I think that He would say, "I don't know, do you think you were doing the right thing or not?" I think, but I'm not sure what He would say back to me. That is hard for me to know.

What would you say back to Him then, if He said that?

[Whispers] I'm not sure...

(At this point Kate starts to get really restless, and it is clear that her attention span is gone. So I end the interview.)

✧

Kate's innocence was so beautiful in this interview. She earnestly explored the idea of what God wants us to do. I was fascinated with her statement that God does not want us to be perfect ~ but good. This is not what the Catholic church taught me. As a recovering Catholic, for years I have been trying to unlearn the dogma of being a sinner and being unworthy of God's love. When I was younger this all got wrapped up in needing to be perfect ~ to please my parents and God. And the guilt that I carried around with me for years might as well have been a five-hundred-pound mantle of rocks on my shoulders.

One Sunday school teacher even taught our class that we should end each day evaluating our sins for the day and ask for God's forgiveness. I wonder if she ever realized how some of us interpreted that teaching. For those of us who grew up feeling as if we were not good enough already, that lesson became an opportunity to wallow in how bad we were each night, another method of self-condemnation. And clearly not the best way to drift off into sleep.

Kate may well grow up a very emotionally healthy person with this belief, as opposed to many of us trying to overcome the curse of perfection or damnation from the religious teachings we grew up with.

CHAPTER 2

THE TEST OF LIFE

CHRISTOPHER HARVEY*
AGE: 10

> THE DIAMOND CANNOT BE POLISHED
> WITHOUT FRICTION, NOR THE MAN
> PERFECTED WITHOUT TRIALS.
>
> ~ CHINESE PROVERB

After I finished interviewing Kate, I went upstairs to Christopher's bedroom. He was at his desk playing a computer game. I watched over his shoulder as he meticulously zapped the last war ships with missiles and, once he was finished, we both sat on the carpet near his bed to do the interview.

Christopher sat cross-legged leaning against his bed. A lanky, handsome child with striking blue eyes and blonde hair, he was a gifted student who, according to his parents, constantly excelled in his class. As he spoke to me, he had a precociously intellectual demeanor. Flanking the wall beside him was a bookcase lined with both children's and adult books. Over one-third of the books focused on baseball. Christopher was a serious fan of the sport. His baseball card collection numbered in the thousands, and he had memorized almost all of them. Over dinner the night

---

*not his real name

before, he quizzed me on baseball statistics in his reserved way, and I was hopelessly ignorant.

✧

If I gave you God's phone number, what would you do with it?

That would be really strange to get God's number. But if you gave me God's phone number, I would call Him. My first question would be: "What do You do with all the people who do not follow Your path of life? Do You just leave them alone and let Satan do his thing with them? Or do You console them and tell them that they haven't been chosen?"

What do you think God might say to that question?

I have been wondering about this question, and I really don't know how God would respond.

Are there any other questions that you would want to ask Him?

I've got lots of questions, such as why does God allow some people to get sick and live short lives while others live long ones? Did He create disease just to kill people?

Is it God or Satan who gives us such strong faults as jealousy, anger or greed? If it is Satan, how does he get the power to do the bad things he does? How did he even become Satan? How did he become evil? Did he just turn away from the Lord and start thinking evil thoughts and doing evil things?

What do you think God's responses might be?

I have no idea how God would answer those questions. But I think Satan has these powers and that God carefully observes how much evil Satan fills us with. This is hard to control, but God keeps watch over it so it doesn't get completely out of hand. This is a big struggle.

I'm also concerned about poor people. Why are there so many poor people, and is this going to be fixed in the future? I'm sure that we always will have kings and presidents and such leaders. But will there be a time when we don't have such rich and such poor? I think about these things lying in bed at night, but I just don't know how God would answer them.

I really think that God has given us a test of life, and if we pass, we go up to the Kingdom of Heaven and live peacefully forever. It's kind of like a report card in life but not exactly; more like a math test. Problem after problem after problem. If you get the problems right, it helps your score. God's got a huge scorecard. If you don't go around angry and hateful or yell at your mom and dad, then you'll get the good grade in the classroom of life.

God will notice when a person is trying to be good. Someone will be trying to follow His path and help others. So He'll look down on them and smile. This gives them good luck. Sometimes people can feel that smile because they get certain signs. Things may not be going well for them and God will change this for a few days.

But you need higher than excellent to get that luck. This is like all the extra stars on your report card.

A report card...?

Yes, God has set it up so that your spiritual report card has been absorbed into yourself. St. Peter sits at the Gate of Heaven and gets a particular reading on each person and either lets him in or banishes him elsewhere.

I'm not sure where those banished people go. I don't

think they are in Hell yet. They might go to Mars or Jupiter or still be around here. They may be wandering around as spirits on the windows listening.

They could be around us causing temptation. They might be what motivate crazy people such as terrorists to do evil things. I think evil spirits are tempting people all the time. Some people are more susceptible to temptation than others, and it is easier for the evil spirits to get them. Then Satan might succeed in getting those people completely.

If these temptations affect some people, they might still have a chance. Even if they've murdered people, they can try to make up for it. If they're willing to repent for their sins, these people really don't deserve to be punished. We've learned this in church. They can still pass the test of life.

Hmmm...Interesting. Is there anything concerning your personal life that you would like to ask God about?

I really don't need to ask God anything about my life. I'm not concerned about myself. I just do normal stuff like fight with my sister. I don't do anything that's really wrong. I get A's in school. But I don't think God is too concerned about grades in school. God is more concerned about people being good.

Any other thoughts?

I've always wondered what Heaven is like. Do you live in your own little house and get everything you need all the time? Or do you live on clouds in the Kingdom of God and you can talk with God anytime you want?

Also do prophets get treated differently in Heaven? Do they get special beds?

Another puzzling thing to me is guardian angels. Do

they tell you what to do and what not to do? I'm not sure they do. I think that they're just there, and maybe sometimes they are messengers of grades back to Heaven if someone has done something really bad, like O.J. Simpson.

And I think about the Garden of Eden. People these days are so greedy. If they ever found Eden, they would probably eat off the Trees of Life and Knowledge. It would be a true test of humans. If whoever finds it is good and kind and has read the Bible, he will not eat from those Trees.

Perhaps the prophets like Jesus ate from these trees before they were born. Jesus might have eaten the fruit because he knew that he had a special job. Then God sent His saviour down.

I have some other questions for God about being born and where we come from, but I want to save a few things so I can go up and ask them after I die. [Laughs]

So you might want to save a few questions for then? (Laughing) Anything else?

God is everywhere on Earth. But He is in some places more than others. It depends on how many good people there are in each of those places speaking to God or thinking about Him or praying.

Another thing ~ God gives fear to everyone, and I think that's rightful. People need to be fearful. If not, I think humans would try to build a stairway up to Heaven.

Then there's the age-old one: "Which came first: the chicken or the egg?" But I wouldn't want to ask God that question now. [Laughs] That's one of the ones that I'll save for when I see Him.

Oh, I need to go. My mother is taking us to the library in five minutes. Thanks.

✧

I always knew that Christopher was a very intelligent child, but this interview truly brought this home to me. It was fascinating how he did not want to ask any personal questions about his life compared with his sister. I wondered if he really did feel that confident that he was living his life in line with what God wishes. Or did he simply not want to be personal? Since in my experience boys don't tend to speak about personal feelings, I was not sure what motivated him to speak as he did.

His perspective on God's smiling or giving fear to everyone was intriguing. Perhaps God does smile on people if that person has a strong connection with Him. I wonder if I have felt that at times ~ times when it felt like life was flowing very smoothly and blissfully, those glimpses of deep spirit in my life.

As for the fear, I'm not sure if God gives that to us. Perhaps He does, but my sense is that fear is part of being human, and God wants us to find the courage to walk through it to discover our potential. That's part of our journey as humans. But...maybe He does give us fear at times so that it can test us.

Christopher's comment about people being "so greedy" amazed me. I wondered how a ten-year-old could already have a perception of our society as being greedy but, then again, Christopher has always been a precocious child.

When I was in Belize volunteering at an ecology center in the remote southwest corner of the country in the winter of 1994-95, I witnessed a very different attitude toward greed. A Mayan village of several hundred people lived just down river from the center. One morning we got word that one of the Mayan men's palm hut on his farm plot had been burned. Without a doubt, the fire had been intentionally started. This was very clear by the way the structure had burned.

While this was not where the man's family lived ~ they

lived in the village ~ this was where he spent most of his time farming. Over time we learned that some of the other villagers had burned his hut because they resented the fact that he was making more money than other villagers. Eladio, the villager whose hut was burned, was leading eco-tourist walks for the center where I was staying and being paid thirty dollars to forty dollars per walk, a relatively high sum for one afternoon's activity and the equivalent of what most Mayans make in six weeks.

Eladio was perceived as being greedy and having more opportunity than his fellow Mayan villagers, and for this he was punished. While in graduate school, I did research on values and read about remote, indigenous villages where resources are always shared equally. Hoarding is very frowned upon, and members of those communities can be ostracized for doing it.

Our mainstream American society treats people like Eladio quite differently. We admire people who have achieved the Great American Dream and have their Jaguars nestled in a country estate garage at night, while people only miles away don't have the resources to feed their children.

I don't think this is what God intended for us. God intended for us to recognize that we live in community and share our resources so that everyone's basic needs are met. We're not good at this on the individual level or the international level in the United States.

Yet I'm an American. I know I can be as individualistic and self-centered as the next person. I have tried to look long and hard inside myself to examine whatever level of greed rests there. What I've discovered is that I'm afraid to really know since I can have a capitalistic mindset like the next American. But I know that it is not the principal modus operandi within me. Actually, since I left my very full-time work in Ann Arbor, Michigan, I've done a splendid job of spending more money than I've made, and I've effectively eaten away most of the money that I inherited. Maybe I don't have that much greed in me after all.

✧

baltimore, maryland
october 1995

dear God...

   i am so upset. i started a spiritual healing course two weeks ago and it is freaking me out. it's called the Awakenings Course and the woman who recommended that i take it told me that it would help me get in touch with my pain and help release it.
   but i've gone two times now and the class terrifies me. there are about twenty-five of us and we all meet in a large sun room off the teacher's house, a room no larger than twenty feet by fifteen. at both classes the teacher guided us to work in partners and release our feelings from the depths of our being. within moments i was surrounded by all these people screaming and crying and really losing it. both nights i just wanted to run so fast out of the room and into the fields outside of the house ~ anywhere to feel safe. if the emotional diarrhea had continued any longer in that room, i was going to clobber the closest screaming person i could get my hands on. this would not have been a good thing. it scares me that i would want to be that violent.
   i decided two days ago that i cannot go back. last night i called one of the assistants and told her that i was not returning. it was an awful conversation. she really tried to pressure me, telling me what i should or should not do. i really wanted to hang up the phone mid-conversation because of how she was treating me. that's it.
   i talked with the teacher today, and she said that she could see that i needed much healing, and she expressed her desire to work with me and be my personal healer ~ only if i do the full course. this truly felt

manipulative. these people really make me angry. it practically feels like a cult. if these people are going to be so controlling ~ i don't need this. i'm quitting the course.

sometimes we try things and they are not right for us, and then we walk away. every person does not need to take the same path to heal or to find God. these people think they are serving up express line enlightenment. it doesn't work that way. whatever spiritual teacher this is and the community she has, it is not for me. fine if it works for some other people, but i am not one of them.

so, God, i'm here again. struggling, still trying to find my way. but that path did not fit. i'm not giving up, though.

i give You my humble love,
Your daughter,

mare

CHAPTER 3

NO NEED FOR IT

EDWARD CURTIS*
AGE: 82

A RADICAL CONVERSION OF
THE NON-POOR
IS NEEDED TODAY.

~ MARIA NEAL

Edward Curtis was an elderly, well-to-do gentleman. He and his wife, Violet, were Judith's houseguests one weekend in late fall. They were making their annual migration from their farm in Connecticut to their winter home in Florida. Edward and Violet had known Judith for years, and this weekend visit was part of their journey south.

Judith invited me to have cocktails with the Curtises the afternoon they arrived. We sat and chatted about stories in the news and their house in Florida. Violet asked me what my work was, and I explained that I was doing part-time work and also starting a book. While I was describing the book to them, I realized that they might be interesting people to interview. So I broached the question, and Violet was very open to it. Edward, on the other hand, was not interested, but I coaxed him into doing it the following morning. I was eager to interview anyone at that time.

To start the interview, I tried to ask Edward a few

---

*not his real name

questions about his life and the work he had been involved in. From the level of conversation that we had the evening before, I had no doubt that he was a conservative man of financial accomplishment. In a reserved tone he related that he had started a chemical company that was significantly successful by the time he retired. His son now runs the company.

Edward was probably only 5′ 7″, but his authoritative manner was of a man who was accustomed to being in charge. His salt and pepper hair belied his age of eighty-two years. He was dressed in his traveling clothes ~ a cashmere sweater and khaki pants.

As Edward and Violet were leaving later that day, I asked him what anonymous name he would like me to use in the book. He looked at me with a sardonic smile and said: "Beelzebub." I shuddered just as he said it. His wife immediately chided him for suggesting it. I gave him a weak smile and responded that I would create another name instead.

✧

If I gave you God's phone number, what would you do with it?

God's phone number? I thought people had that. That's what we have religion for.

If someone were to give me a phone number on a piece of paper and tell me it's God's ~ I'm not a good one to be asked that question. I'm afraid that I'm not very religious. I think if I had to describe my religion with one word, I'd say ~ what is that word? ~ oh, yes, agnostic.

If somebody gave me such a number, I would put it with my old prayer books in a drawer somewhere. I'd just leave it there. I don't think I'd be tempted to pull it out later.

Would you ever be tempted to pull it out and just look at it, at least?

I don't think so. I'm not afraid of dying. I think fear of dying is why most people want to try to communicate with God. But I would not use the number.

I may change, but I don't know. I'm an admirer of religion. I think it does a lot of people a lot of good. But it is not something that I use. When I was a young boy, I might have used such a number. But I could not say now what I would have used it for. I'd have to give that a lot of thought. It's the farthest thing from my mind.

I know it sounds terrible. But it doesn't mean that I don't have a lot of respect for religion. I do. I think it influences people for the better. But I don't have a need for it. Sorry.

You don't need to apologize to me or anyone else about your beliefs.

I think it's important for people to have some kind of a routine that they adhere to. Routines such as treating others as you would be treated and so on. And I think that most people do have such routines. Otherwise it would be pretty chaotic. I guess you could call it a code of ethics. And some people have a code of ethics because they're afraid they'll go to Hell if they don't. And that's probably a good thing. Makes them behave better, perhaps.

I know a lot of people think it's heretical to have that kind of belief. It's not the kind of thing I talk about with people. I don't brag about it. I'm not proud of it. It's just the way I am.

It can be upsetting to people. It would be very upsetting to my father and mother if they heard me talk like that. And it probably would be hard for my brother also. I have one brother who is still living. He's very religious. He goes to church and he talks about it quite a bit.

I don't like to talk about this with devout Catholics because it can seem that I think I'm better than they are. I certainly don't feel that way. I just have a different philosophy about it. They're not usually broad-minded about these things. Actually, I think it's just as hard for people in any religion.

[Meekly] I'm not a very good subject for this.

No, you are a very good subject for this.

Frankly, the God that is seen in most religions is something I just don't have. I have a great deal of respect for the more or less orderly process of ecology and astronomy and so on. But I don't think it is the provenance of some supernatural force. The planets, the universes and so on.

And I don't think Jesus Christ was there when it all started. I think He's an image that many people use to help them overcome their fear of death. He gives them an incentive to act in an orderly way. And I think it's very good.

About His being the Son of God and all that, I think the Moslems have just as much right to their idea of the way things happened. Or any one of a hundred different religions.

I'm sure there have been others like Christ. Take the cult leader in Japan who was responsible for the gas in the subway: I'm sure that his people put him in some kind of a category like that. And to the extent that these people don't injure other people, they're entitled to that, I suppose. But when they start spreading lethal gas, then they're not. Then they're bad.

I don't think Jesus Christ would have done something like that. He was a good man. I think that there have been many good men, though.

I really have no image of God. If we have a God, I don't know how far His influence would extend. Would it go to the moon and beyond? They'd be entitled to have their

God, too.

I've never thought about there being a God on the moon!

Sure. So, yes, I'm an agnostic. But I haven't been this way all of my life. I was born a Catholic. I went to parochial school until I was about ten. I was an altar boy at one time because that's what my mother wanted me to be. Since I've done my own thinking, though, I've gradually come into being an agnostic.

I don't think about it incessantly, either. But this is now the way I feel. I would say I've felt this way many, many years. I'm not going to start a new religion to advocate my point of view. I know it's not very widely shared. But it's good for me, I think.

✧

Edward was very clear on his views. While many might not agree with him, I found his beliefs interesting. More than anything, though, I felt sad for Edward since I believe that he is missing out on a very significant part of life ~ developing a connection with God. It is my spiritual beliefs that give me hope and inspire me. Knowing that God loves me, as I believe so strongly that He does, helps me live my life more positively and with greater inner strength.

Perhaps Edward was so self-confident and assured in his life that he did not need God as I do. But I cannot help but believe that everyone needs God. Or perhaps it is the other way around. Perhaps God needs us. And if more of us recognized this, then the world would be a more positive place.

But Edward's life seems to work with his agnostic views. He seemed content with his place in the world. Having such great financial success certainly helps support this.

Edward was similar to so many corporate types I've

met. They are intelligent people, but many seem to have pursued education of the head and achievement in the purse but not education of the spirit.

The Dalai Lama teaches about secular humanism, saying that we do not have to pursue religious or spiritual teachings if we did not want to. Instead, if we all focused on kindness and compassion, this in itself would make a world of difference. Perhaps he is right. However, I still feel so comforted with my spiritual belief that there is a God and He loves me unconditionally.

I do wonder if Edward's views will change when he is truly on the verge of death.

CHAPTER 4

I'VE BEEN RECYCLED

VIOLET CURTIS*
AGE: 68

SEARCH FOR GOD WHERE YOU LOST HIM.

~ TONY DE MELLO

fter Edward Curtis finished his interview, his wife Violet was available to talk with me.

Violet was very personable and chatty. She started by telling me some of her life story. She was originally born in England to an affluent family, but the British Army took over their estate when WWII started and the family was forced to move to London. When the bombs started dropping on London, her parents decided to send Violet and her three brothers to Pennsylvania to be cared for by an American couple. So at the age of ten, Violet was shipped to the New World on a boat with more than fifteen hundred children, all destined to live in the safety of the United States with adoptive parents.

The United States became Violet's home. She never returned to live in England. Her American parents were rather wealthy, and she attended boarding school during her high school years. Choosing to skip college, she moved to New York City after high school and got involved in

*not her real name

publishing. She first married at the age of twenty-two, and Edward Curtis was her third husband. I never did find out how many children she had.

Violet was a very attractive older woman with a practical yet aristocratic way about her. I could see that she was a kind but strong woman. I imagined that she had been quite beautiful and had many suitors when she was young. Much as I wanted to ask her more about her life, I knew that she and her husband had to leave soon, so we launched into the interview.

✧

If I gave you God's phone number, what would you do with it?

I would call immediately. Never put off what you can do right away.

I would ask Him how did this Creation get so screwed up? Is this how You pictured it ~ just total chaos taking over?

I think there have been many mistakes made in the Creation, one of them being that Man and Woman were not created equal. That was a big mistake. They are actually supposed to be equal, but Man has made it his world rather than their world and that's where things started going wrong.

I'm sure God would be feeling that I was very presumptuous to ask these questions, but I hope that He would know that I wouldn't mean to be irreverent.

I'm also hoping that God is a man because I don't think a woman would do this. I think that if God were a woman, there'd be more sensitivity as to what would go on among people.

How do you think God would respond to your question about the world's being so screwed up?

He may tell me that it's none of my business. He may say that He has this great plan and that the strongest will eventually survive. The rest will fall by the wayside as other animals like the dinosaurs have done. Maybe we will also fall by the wayside if we can't get it together. Or we might just destroy ourselves, which we're well on the way to doing.

Or He may not think that He needs to answer me.

But if He did...

For me to get into God's mind is very difficult since I don't look upon God as a person. I look upon God as a Creator that has made all these things work ~ plants and animals and the moon, all that sort...I don't consider Him as a man doing and thinking about "manly" things. I think that's making it too simple.

Are there any other questions that you would want to ask this entity that you call God?

I would like to know if we are the only one out here or are there many others that He's also experimenting with? I hope there are some others because we can't be the ultimate. We are so-o-o bad. Our history is just terrible.

And if there is something else out there, will we ever meet them? If so, will it be more war rather than cooperation? We always seem to feel that we have to conquer somebody. It's been that way all through our history. Tribes conquered other tribes until they banded together and made countries and now they're still trying to conquer each other. If this is what's going to happen in our space exploration efforts, then we're really in trouble because we're not bright enough to conquer others out there in space.

I'm sure that there are others out there. I can't believe that we are the only people in this whole universe that have any intelligence.

How do you think God would respond to that question? That's a tough one.

He may say, "You're not very intelligent." [Laughs] It's hard to talk about God because some people are absolutely certain that God has a beard and He's a very noble man. I'm not so sure that God isn't someone who just plays games.

God has such tremendous power. But I don't think He uses it. I think He just lets things go. If He had power, He wouldn't have let the Holocaust go on. If that's what happened, then He's playing games. If He's doing it for a reason, I don't find Him a nice person.

What do you think God would say to that?

He'd say: "You don't understand my ultimate plan."

But I really can't see how God can be so all-caring and all-powerful and let perfectly innocent children and adults be killed. What I find so extraordinary is that so many awful things have happened. There was an article in the paper today ~ they found a grave that's two thousand years old in China where thousands of men were buried alive. How can that be allowed to happen? Just because one man fought over this piece of territory and his soldiers were pawns in this whole thing, when they lost, they were buried alive.

Now I don't find that a very caring person who would let that happen. And that was two thousand years ago. Recently in Bosnia, soldiers were just slaughtering men thinking it's nothing but a rabbit hunt. Over six thousand people were killed.

That would not happen if I were running something unless I enjoyed watching it or I was doing an experiment. Or perhaps I was teaching them a lesson. But I don't think I could let that happen.

So you're saying that your image of God is not that of a grandfatherly figure and that God may be conducting a large experiment?

He may or He may not be. He could have started something and now He's just looking at it thinking: "What have I started? But it's interesting...Might as well just keep it going."

The tribes of South America considered the sun as a God. But there again, they had to appease the God. God was almighty and very wrathful. They had to appease by killing virgins, which I find awful. God is not something that has been an endearing thing in the eyes of many people of this world.

Yes...Any other questions that you might want to ask?

I'd like to ask Him if time is on our side, and will we ever see the light and become one world? Certainly not in my lifetime and certainly not for another five hundred years, I'll bet. And even then, will we end up with a super race of people who have annihilated everybody else? That perhaps is not the answer, either.

Would you be curious and want to ask God about life after death? That's a large question for most of us.

[Laughs] I could ask Him that. I could ask anything, it's my nickel. [More laughter] I cannot imagine that He's going to take all these people who have been on Earth and put them or recycle them somewhere else. I think He sends us back here.

I have a feeling I've been recycled. I go to certain places and can almost describe what they look like before I get there. I was in Topkapi, Istanbul, and when I walked into the palace there I became quite upset because it was in such disarray. I distinctly remember it feeling like it was my house. But it was terribly unkempt. I sat down at a window overlooking the Bosporus River, and it felt like I had seen that same view many times. It's the sultan's palace, a very famous place.

Some of my friends have had past-life regressions. One had been an Egyptian oarsman in one of those slave galleys. I have this one Jewish friend who found out that he was an Aztec boy who was sacrificed in one of his past lives. That he could be anything but a Jew was extraordinary to him.

So you find it hard to believe that God would take all these people and have room for all of them somewhere else? And that maybe we're recycled here?

Maybe not everybody's recycled. I hate to think of God being biased about people, but it could be that certain people are so bad they don't get recycled. Or it might be the opposite. If you're so bad, you're definitely coming back to get it right.

It's a fascinating thought that maybe you were an Indian at one time and now you're going to be a Russian prince or a hard laborer. Do all these past lifetimes eventually make up your character?

These past-life memories are extraordinary, or maybe it's just a fantastic imagination. Nothing can be proven by it. I find that fascinating. Perhaps we keep coming back again and again until we get it right.

But I don't see that people are any better today than they were. If you read history and how people lived and fought, they don't seem to be any different. So we're not making much progress.

It must be God's wish that we are so aggressive and we have great biases toward other people. Maybe we are born that way. Maybe it is in our gene makeup. To get this far, we had to be aggressive in order to survive. It seems to me there should be a certain point in the evolution of the world that you don't need to be aggressive to fix problems. But we're not there yet.

So maybe I'm agnostic. I don't believe there is one person up there overseeing this whole mess.

But do you think there's something or nothing?

Certainly there is something that caused the Big Bang ~ chemicals of some sort. But whether God is just a man or groups of chemicals...We've tried to simplify things scientifically to where we think they can be explained, but I think it's much more complicated than that.

People used to have an absolute fit when an eclipse of the sun would happen. They thought that was the end of the Earth. Now we know it's just the shadow of the moon. People do learn. I don't think we can explain the Big Bang yet although we're getting close to it. I really do think we have to continue to research outer space, and if we do find out how this all came about, it's going to be a terrible thing for the people who are very religious. Everything they believed in...

Or it could be the opposite?

Or it could be the opposite. Those that don't believe are now going to have to. Either way ~ bad for a lot and good for a lot.

Is there anything else that you would pose to this...this mass of chemicals?

I think we are our own destiny. People ask God's permission to do this or that or to be safe. But I think that's not right. I think it's an egotistical way of looking at life ~ to think that you, one little person, are going to be looked after by God. That God is going to say, "I'm going to take care of you." I don't think that's true. I think it's just hit or miss and luck and chaos. Sometimes you're in the right place and sometimes you're not.

I think I'd ask Him whether this has to go on like this forever. "At one point will you put a stop to this and give people better reason?"

It's an interesting subject, and of course it's been talked about forever and will continue to be because it's a mystery.

Certainly is...Violet, can you tell me a little about your religious background?

I was born in England, and my only religious background until I was ten was to give my favorite toy on Christmas Eve to the toy box. We did not go to church. The Church of England is the state church, and a lot of people go and a lot of people don't go. It's not like the Catholic Church where you had to go.

Then I came over to this country in WWII where a family took us for the duration of the war. They would take us to an Episcopal Church, but the minister was so bad. You couldn't understand him because he was an alcoholic. It was just ridiculous, so we weren't forced to go to church.

The only church that I felt had anything going for it was the Quaker Church. That's where you do not have a minister telling you what to do. But I don't go to Quaker meetings that often.

In fact every time I do go into a church with a friend, I come out so angry at what they're feeding people that I just never go back until someone drags me back again.

This past summer we were on a Smithsonian trip in Europe to learn about medieval art and history. We went to these large cathedrals in small villages and learned how much work was spent on constructing these buildings by people who barely subsisted on what they were growing. And all the wars that came back and forth over those villagers' land, and yet they kept having to build these cathedrals. All to save their souls. They were really intimidated into doing these things.

I felt it was just terrible by the end of the trip. If Jesus Christ were the Son of God, he would absolutely have had a fit over what he had started. I think Christ was a simple man, and he would not have envisioned these enormous cathedrals in little villages that the people still have to keep up.

They're such works of art yet such suffering went into the construction of them. Is there anything else that you would like to add?

Yes, the one thing that I've learned in life ~ I don't know whether you can deem it to be religious or not ~ but nothing is forever. Don't ever think that just because you're leading a nice life it means that this will go on indefinitely. Because tomorrow it may be all gone. So don't panic when things go wrong.

✧

I was very intrigued with Violet's thoughts about reincarnation. I also have experienced certain visions that could only be from past lives. There is no other way to explain it. They clearly were not dreams.

Each time I have experienced one of these visions, it was during a time of profound inner stillness: once when I was receiving a massage and another time when I was doing very slow leg exercises in a class. In the first one I experienced, I was standing along the edge of an open circle in a forest, and I was participating in a ceremony at night. There were candles or torches at specific points in the grove, and the atmosphere was charged with a powerful solemnity.

The second time I experienced one, I was with a small group of tensely silent people by a small fire in the dark of night. It seemed as though we were waiting for a signal to mount our horses and leave ~ perhaps to battle ~ I don't know. I got the sense that we needed to be extremely still. The only perceptible sounds were the horse bits jangling near us. Both of these remembrances were very emotionally charged. Perhaps that is why the memories became so etched in my soul-body.

There is another pattern in my life that could quite possibly be traced to past-life experiences. For years I had an inexplicable fear of physical intimacy with men whenever I was feeling particularly anxious.

I would lie in bed in college and hear roommates having sex in the next room. Not only was it irritating that they had awakened me, but my whole body would tense up while I heard the sounds. It was as though I were afraid of being sexually attacked. I am certain that I had never been sexually violated in this lifetime, but my body seemed to have a visceral memory of being attacked.

One day while I was still living in Michigan, I received a massage from someone new. A friend had recommended her. As soon as she started working on my shoulders, she launched into telling me about a past life of mine she could see. She said that it was during the Victorian times and I lived in a castle. I wore the high-necked collars and the fancy dresses of that time. She could see that I was the lady of the castle. I was a good horseback rider and also knew a great deal about herbs and healing. Women would come to me for healing.

As the massage continued, she gave me more details. I was married to a man who basically raped me over and over again. In her words, sex was quite unpleasant. And I had an abortion and died. That is just how she stated it: "You had an abortion and you died."

I remember getting off that massage table and reeling emotionally. I had come for a massage to find some peace at a very stressful point in my life. Instead, I went home with not only my present challenging life situation but another one that was quite plausible to try to process.

I was open to what she had told me. Perhaps it was true. My lifelong interest in horses and medicinal plants may well have stretched to earlier than this lifetime. And I always felt as if my life has been one of aristocratic privilege. It would make sense that I had experienced similar lifetimes. Perhaps my soul has memories of being sexually violated over and over again and this has been viscerally etched into my subconscious.

Several years after that massage, I went out on a date with a doctor to whom I was quite attracted. We had met at a dance, and initially I thought we had many things in common. But after one phone conversation and one date, I was very put off by the man's comments to me.

At the end of the date, he told me that when he first saw me that night, he wanted to rip off my clothes and have wild sex but after spending the evening together, he wanted to make passionate love to me all night instead. This was far too much information for me. There were several other things he said to me also that let me know that he perceived women only as sex objects.

As I drove home that night, I knew I did not feel safe with him. A deep instinct in me encouraged me to stay away. I wrote him a letter several days later to communicate my feelings, and we had a difficult phone conversation shortly afterward. I got the sense that he had no idea how he came across to women. We never spoke again.

I talked with a psychic friend at the time and she told me that I had been with a man like that in a past life, and after I died I swore that I would never again be with another one. It may well have been the lifetime I was living in the castle. Perhaps that information was encoded into my soul so that when I was reborn, the instinct surfaced to protect me.

CHAPTER 5

BRING HIM ON!

JOHN TERLAZZO
AGE: 41

WE HAVE BEEN LOVED BY GOD
FROM BEFORE THE BEGINNING.

~ JULIAN OF NORWICH

John Terlazzo is a poet and musician. I met him in the early fall of 1995 at a weekend poetry retreat he led on the organic farm where he and his family lived. I was one of nine participants that weekend. It was a rustic, community-oriented event where we all slept in our tents in the back field and helped do dishes when we were not playing with words in creative ways.

I enjoyed getting to know John as he gently pushed and prodded us to express our voice on paper. He was a short, intense but gentle man who took his art very seriously. He had memorized many of his poems, and when he recited them, his depth and presence awed me. It was clear that he was a true artist with a passion for expressing himself.

John was an artist who did 'bread and butter' work to support his creative efforts. Sometimes he was compensated for a music concert or poetry reading, but mostly his income came from house painting and commissions for murals, among other odd jobs. When we first met, his wife was fighting breast cancer and was working only part time, so there was more responsibility on John to bring income in.

John and I stayed in touch after that retreat. We collaborated in a reading at one of the Baltimore poetry spots later in the fall. I felt that it was quite an honor to be reading my work alongside such a talented person.

During the retreat, I had told John about the book, and he expressed a desire to be interviewed, so we set it up after our reading.

✦

If I gave you God's phone number, what would you do with it?

Well, I'd have to call. Partly it would be curiosity. But another part would be the idea of hooking up to some natural voice speaking in English for the God Energy. There is this thing about God Energy. We're swimming in it. It's swimming in us. I'd have to see if I could really talk with this.

What do you think you would say?

Hmm... [pause] ...That would depend on when you asked me. If you asked me today ~ this may be too mundane ~ but I would want to ask God why so much of our lives, my life, are ruled by money. I do five different things for a living, and the ones that I do the very best are the ones I don't get to do often enough and don't get to make enough money doing. I've been asking this God Energy this question a lot of times. The last couple of days I've been painting the roof of a barn. I make my own hours and all that, but it's not what I do. It's not who I am. I want an answer to that question.

If this God Energy gave you an answer, what do you think that answer might be?

You know...I guess the answer's pretty obvious. It would be: "Hey, I didn't design it that way. Other people did that, and I may be able to tell you how it's going to turn out, but this is your trip. You've got to do this. You've got to figure it out."

I guess that's always true. But it's strange to me that there are so many great poets walking around on the Earth, and only some are making a living. There are so many that are struggling so hard. Yet the number-one-grossing business in this country is weaponry. There's something there that's really out of whack.

Would you want to ask God about this?

I wouldn't ask God why it is that weapons are such a popular business. I know that that's not God's doing. I think I know the answer ~ it is that profit is more important to this culture than God.

A whole culture can be based on profit because people are unhappy. Somehow they think that attaining more will change that and make them happier. Maybe I would ask God what could I do about it. But I don't know. [Deep sigh]

I could do what the Berrigans did and go into weapons plants and destroy those guns and get thrown into jail. I don't know if that would answer anything. I really honor them for having done that, but I don't know if that changes things.

I can try to find time and space to make more art. I do think that a person making a poem, speaking it out loud, even if it's in their bedroom and nobody else is around, is a very healing thing. I think it's a very mystical thing.

There is an energy to speaking our poetry, really Speaking with a capital S. I think we have to ask ourselves what is this stuff, this energy, and also really revel in the mystery of what that is.

Is this what you call the God Energy, this stuff that you are talking about?

I think it is. This spirit is in everything. It's in you. It's in the bricks. It's in the trees. And it's so much more that that. And yet, I really get tongue-tied at this point because it's... [pause] ...this Being, the Big Being is all around, and we're in it.

When we get caught up in the daily struggle of paying bills, it's real easy to lose track of that. To not recognize that you're eating miracles all the time.

So I have a mixed feeling about someone's saying, "Here's God's number, you can just call up." On one hand I feel like I'm already right there in the middle of it. I should be able to get all the answers. They are internalized. They're here.

And then again, there's a part of me that says, "Yeah, I want to not only get the phone number, I want the address, fax number...email. I want to look into this face and see the face that's behind the face."

So many times in my life I've wanted to see that face in a really joyful way. I'm doing some great dance, and I really want to be grateful about it. Then there're times when ~ I've been there a bit lately ~ I want to see this face because I just want to say, "Come on, you know, what is this? Give me a break and make it clear!"

You're talking about being in the throes of the trials and tribulations of our human existence...I really wonder if having such a number would make our trials any easier. I don't know.

Well, I think the big mistake that's been made about God in so many church philosophies is that they think they understand God. They think they know what and who God is and what God looks like. And I think that's a big mistake right there.

We're not supposed to get this. It's supposed to be a mystery. And the fact is that it's the mystery that I really love. I really love the fact that we can spend all of our lifetimes trying to figure this out and put a name on it. And it can't be done. At some point, when we see the real vision, there's just no way it could be explained in human terms. No name would make it. No words could describe it.

It might actually be that if we dialed the phone number, the top of our heads would completely explode!

Hmmm...It sounds like it would be very problematic for you to consider that there is such a phone number because your perception of God and God Energy is beyond what any phone line could reach.

Yeah, that's clearly true. Although it's still a great fantasy. I'd like to be able to call up God and really ask him about my life and what it is about. I like to think that it could be some sort of very friendly, warm, intimate conversation.

I guess my wide-open vision of God is so far outside of any artificial constructs that the phone number concept is hard. I envision that when I truly see God, at the end of this life or however many lives it takes, at that point there won't be any need for me to make conversation. In that space everything is answered.

When I die, I don't see Heaven as some really boring space. Instead, I see an endless chain of clarity, understanding and wonder. Maybe like the best imaginable art, and it just keeps happening. Every corner you turn, there is more of it happening.

Some people may think my vision is very naïve. I guess I would ask them the question: "Why would you seem to think that, given the amount of miracle that exists around us all the time, why would you think there would be such a thing as limits?"

I think our scientifically based society has done us a disservice. Now that we have scientific definitions for things, we cease to realize how incredible these things are. Look at water. Water is liquid energy. It's always been there. It cleanses us. It's a phenomenal substance. Yet we take it for granted.

We just turn on a faucet, we wash and then we turn it off, and it doesn't really mean anything to us. Yet, if you think about it, washing your face alone can be an incredibly sacred act ~ if you can just be with it while you do it instead of thinking of twenty other things.

And I'm not pretending that I'm really good at being with it. But there's incredible mystery in that. To just say it's two atoms of hydrogen and one of oxygen, what a disservice we do not only to the water but even worse to ourselves. We dismiss this phenomenon, this natural spiritual reality as if it were the paper we wrap around burgers at McDonald's.

Even the paper around the burgers could be a mystery, too. It's a great concept that all of this is God Energy here on this plane. And when we leave here, it can only get better. Can't get worse ~ or maybe it could?

I don't think so. I don't adhere to any one system of belief, but reincarnation makes sense to me, the individual spirit moving in and out of physical forms. Some may think of it as bad news. But I think we just have to work through whatever suffering we have again and again and again until we get it figured out.

But ultimately there's got to be a space where there is clarity. I don't mean that in a desperate way, like I'll fall down now and cry if there isn't. I just mean, given all the miracle that's going on around us all the time, there's got to be more wonder than what we can perceive at this time.

A couple of months ago, a guy with Jesus pamphlets stopped me in the street saying, "Are you ready...Are you ready to meet Jesus?" And it would have been real easy to get aggravated and brush the guy off. But I thought about it and I said, "Well, yeah, you know, I'm really ready. Bring Him on! It'd be really great. Let's do it!"

I don't remember if we got into much of a conversation. I've had this conversation with a lot of people. But Jesus, Krishna, Vishnu, any name you put on it, it's the same stuff, just bring it on! You know, I want it!

What I mean is I want the clarity. But of course I know I have the clarity. There is always that dichotomy. A Zen teacher I had in New York would teach, "You know, it's not something you have to get to, to be Buddha. It's not that you have to sit zazen for fifty years and then maybe you get to be Buddha: the minute that you sit zazen, you're Buddha. Twenty years sitting is twenty years Buddha. Twenty minutes sitting is twenty minutes of Buddha."

He wasn't saying when you get up and then walk away you're not Buddha because you're not doing this form of practice. He was just saying that in the conscious act of doing zazen, or Tai Chi, yoga or any other discipline, you are Buddha. You are clarity, complete clarity. It's all right there inside.

It's just there's some part of us that's considerably unbalanced. Consider how a few businessmen get together and say to each other, "If we sold guns to this side and sold guns to that side, then we couldn't lose." The fact that they couldn't comprehend that all these people would die means everybody loses, including them. This type of human action shows that we're really out of whack.

But at the same time every one of us, including any one

of those businessmen, could stop and realize the clarity.

That would be a great strategy. But how to get them to do it?

How to get me to do it! I know I could access this clarity. I know that God dwells inside me, and I know that I have the answers to any question. And yet, I walk around all the time banging into doors, tripping over steps, kicking myself again, feeling angry over something that's meaningless, jealous, arrogant or greedy.

Somewhere at the center ~ there's a seed, there's a real gift. I just have a hard time finding it while I'm feeling wretched.

You're not the only one. Hmmm...If you really could call, is there anything you'd want God to say to you?

[Long pause] ...The tender answer is probably one that I'd need to hear the most. I would want God to tell me that I'm loved ~ that I'm really loved. I would really like that.

Beyond that I would want God to say: "Yes, you're right about poetry, just go forward and do it and don't do anything else. And everything you need will be there. Yes, you're right to believe that poetry is inherent in all human beings, art is inherent in all human beings. And yes, that it is a worthwhile thing to spend your life trying to encourage people to make flesh out of their words, to encourage people to understand that they hold this spiritual wonder inside them and they can Speak with a capital S. It would feed them to do that."

That's very thoughtful. You're really speaking some of your passion.

Yeah. Thanks for giving me the opportunity. I have read

that there were shamans in tribal cultures that wrote poetry and healed people with those words. I mean, that's not some fantasy, it's a very real thing and that can exist now. I've seen it done.

There is something very mystical about the poem. People don't usually applaud after a poem. It's usually silence until the person finishes at the end of the night and walks off the stage. I think there's a sense of the sacred around poetry. There should be, I mean.

Where do you think poems come from?

Well, if you believe that creation is unfolding all the time and you're part of it, as I do, as opposed to a very literal theological idea that creation happened in seven days' time, you start to understand that you are doing this thing interdependently with the Great Being. You're not just along for the ride. Then you can understand that when you go into a poem or piece of music or a piece of art as an experience, it becomes mystical.

It can be done with anything: scat jazz music as much as saying the rosary at a former concentration camp. There is just as much God in both places, and we can connect with it. And it gets filtered through whoever we are at the time. Sometimes I go through some of my old poetry and am surprised that at the age of nineteen, I actually understood something.

I love some of Nikos Kazantsakis's work. He wrote The Last Temptation of Christ. It was made into a movie, but unfortunately many people misinterpreted his work. His notion was that it wasn't God's responsibility to save Man. It was Man's responsibility to save God. What he meant by that was that it was our joy and also our duty to live life in such a way that the passion within us would contact the passion within all things. Our passion would contact God and pull the spiritual world into the physical world and make it evident in front of our eyes.

What I hear you saying is that it is for humans to remember God, to bring God back.

Yes ~ to want God so bad that we burn away the layers of those things that keep us from God. A lot of those things are very obvious. I mean, if you really want God, smash your television. If you really want God, start to honor the body and feed it well.

I'm not pretending to be the master of all this stuff; I screw up all the time. But if you really want God, I mean, don't...

[Long pause]

I just get to a point where I can't talk about it.

That's okay. Can you tell me a little about your upbringing? How were you raised?

Catholic. I feel very grateful for that. I know that a lot of people have suffered a lot at the hands of the Catholic Church, but there's been some greatness there for me. I really loved all the mystical stories as a kid in Catholic school. They really filled me up, stories about St. Francis and people like that. It was so obvious to me that when somebody like St. Francis would come forward and talk about the wolf being his brother, he meant it. He meant that we clearly are not above anything else in nature, we are one.

In the Middle Ages there were lots of wonderful, incredible monks who were very much tuned in to the essence of their tradition. Monks like St. Francis and people from other beliefs. The Sufis as a part of Islam and those in Judaism committed to the Kabbalah, and in Shinto and Taoism ~ the essence is there in all these different traditions.

The real mystics are the guys who meet each other on the road, no matter what tradition they are from, and they know. They know they share the truth. It's unfortunate, though, that they usually are a small percentage of the larger group. So you have fundamentalist Christians and you have fundamentalist Muslims and they want to kill each other. It's incredible.

So anyway, I was raised Catholic, but I've read a lot and I've looked into a lot of spiritual traditions and philosophies, and again what I see in all of these things is the same essence.

Interesting. So you were raised Catholic and then you basically just started exploring on your own beyond that.

Yeah, and I see all the threads that pull it all together that show me that God is one being and It's in everything. There is only God. There is no devil. And anything that is screwed up in the world and bitter and evil and uncomfortable, it's just us being out of balance. And it's a matter of us getting our act together and becoming responsible.

If we recognize that all is God, then the manufacturers of weapons have no chance of making a profit. You don't shoot God. You don't go over the hill or over the ocean and put a machine gun in somebody's chest and kill them. These manufacturers will go do something else for a living.

I don't feel pessimistic about these things because if I can have these thoughts, then there have got to be millions of other people who have thoughts that are a lot more powerful than this. So there's a lot of hope.

It just takes more of us trying to figure it out and trying to encourage more conscious living. I'm feeling like maybe you're reaching a resolution here. Is there anything else you want to share regarding this phone number?

I think I'd want to know where to go with all this stuff that I feel so strongly about. Why am I filled with such powerful feelings and beliefs if I'm not to be called upon to set them free? Why are people like me made to burn so much?

Yeah, I can give some poetry readings here and there, and that sets it free. And God willing and me willing at the same time, I'll get to do a lot more of that.

But there are some days when I think, "Okay, if this is all there is, if You're not going to let me set this stuff free more than I've been able to, then maybe I'm ready to lie down and die. Maybe it's okay."

And that's not like me to feel that way. I don't want to lie down and die. I really want to dance and dance and dance and then dance some more. If I die, it's okay, but I don't want it to be because I'm dissatisfied that I haven't been able to get my words out. And I've known that dance a lot of my life.

And you're ready to dance more. This is what I really hear. So how would God respond to that?

... [Long pause] ...Appropriately.

✧

John Terlazzo's interview was a powerful one. There were so many things he said that prompted me to think.

For one, I admired his courage to step up to the evangelist on the street and state forthrightly that he was ready to meet Jesus ~ right there in that moment.

I'm not always sure that I'm ready to show up in front of Christ or God and have them see me completely. Perhaps part of me is ashamed of some of my weaknesses, my fears, my idiosyncrasies. But John's life and his poetry exemplify someone who has not been afraid to be present. And I could picture him standing right up to Jesus Christ and openly conversing and then probably basking in incredible love. People who have had near-death experiences talk about the intensity of the love that they felt after their consciousness left their body ~ so much more than anything they have felt before. I do wonder if I am afraid of being bowled over by such intense love, as I imagine God and Jesus Christ have for us. But what a silly fear.

John did seek answers about why his life is so hard. I imagine that most artists might ask this question since life seems to be so much more intense for them with their sensitivity and passion to create, often in a world that does not appreciate them.

It has also been said that deeply spiritual people face more challenging life experiences generally. Some of the most spiritual people I've met have lived extremely hard lives, starting with child abuse and being physically assaulted in their adulthood. These people are truly tested. And John was both an artist and spiritual so it could well be that his path in life was not destined to be simple.

One compelling belief that John had was that poetry, all art, can come from that divine place within us where a part of us is merged with God. I do believe that each of us carries a piece of it. And when we create from that place within us and release it into the world, we send our love that is God's love that resonates universally. I loved how John expressed this.

His statement that we are not supposed to get the mystery made me laugh since I was trying so hard to understand. Here I was pounding the streets trying to talk to people so that I can figure it all out, and John is saying that I'll never get it in all of my lifetimes until maybe...who knows when? And at that point, I imagine I could not even put it into words. I guess I'm stubborn enough to still try.

I could really resonate with John's term "God Energy." In 1992, I went to India to study yoga for several weeks. One of the teachings that the Indian instructors impressed on us was that everything is divine. Everything embodies God.

For weeks after I returned from India, I would look at trash cans on the streets of Ann Arbor and imagine them as divine. It was quite a switch from seeing them as dirty, smelly containers for our waste. I remember arriving at my office feeling like I carried more of the divine with me each morning. But as the weeks passed and life's distractions stole my attention, my perceptions of the objects around me returned to the mundane.

One thing that I did not agree with John about was that there is no devil and that all the screwed-up aspects of the world are our fault. Certainly humans can and have created some nasty situations, but I believe that there are negative entities, some more powerful than others, that are constantly trying to trip us up and push us to do dark deeds. I remember talking with a friend years ago about the concept of "possession." This man had known a Catholic priest in France who witnessed an exorcism. According to the man I spoke with, invisible forces had pulled up the priests conducting the exorcism along with the possessed woman twenty to twenty-five feet above the pews in the church. They were all dangling in mid-air near the front of the church. For how long, I do not know. The story was very unsettling to hear. I can't remember whether they considered the exorcism successful or not. I now believe that some of the most difficult people I've met were probably possessed. It may not be that uncommon.

CHAPTER 6

IT'S ALL A CONTINUUM

SARAH DORN*
AGE: 27

...IT'S THE PERSON CALLED ME, CHRISTINE, THAT
GOD IS MOST INTERESTED IN. I NOW KNOW
THAT I'M NOT ONLY SINFUL, BUT ALSO UNIQUE
AND PRECIOUS. I AM LEARNING TO GIVE GOD
MY SECRET, SHAMEFUL SELF IN ORDER THAT
I MIGHT DISCOVER THE BITS OF MYSELF WHICH
AREN'T THAT BAD AFTER ALL.

~ CHRISTINE REID

In December of 1996, a good friend from graduate school invited me up to New York City for a New Year's Eve party. I was happy to take a break from Baltimore for two days. I had moved out of Judith's house in late November to farm-sit on a nearby farm estate that was in the process of being sold. While it was an adventure living alone on a 280-acre farm, I longed for a break.

My friend worked in the arts in New York so there was an eclectic mix of people at her party. One woman there was a striking, dark-haired actress in her late twenties named Sarah Dorn. Sarah and I struck up a conversation about God and my book. The more Sarah talked, the more I

---

*not her real name

realized that beneath her poise was an anxious young woman trying to figure out her life. She was presently taking pre-med classes to apply for medical school. After listening to her for a while, I asked her if she would like to be interviewed, and she was interested.

We arranged to meet at her parents' apartment in the Upper West Side of Manhattan the following afternoon. Sarah was home visiting her parents for Chanukah.

Sarah's father was a very successful surgeon; thus, her parents lived in a posh apartment building in Manhattan. When I arrived at the building, there were doormen and even an elevator man. I felt a bit underdressed in my blue jeans and heavy overcoat as I walked by several very sophisticated women in the lobby.

Sarah welcomed me into an ornate living room dotted with original pieces of art. It was evident that she had grown up in privileged circumstances.

✦

If I gave you God's phone number, what would you do with it?

If someone gave me a phone number and said it was God's, I would probably put it on my bureau and stare at it for a few days trying to decide whether to use it or not. I'd have to think about all the different motives I'd have for talking to God.

I have a lot of different ideas about God. I was originally taught that God was this animated male figure with a white beard sitting up in the clouds somewhere. But I have a hard time with that image now. I tend to think of God as more of a warm spirit out there that I appeal to.

I see God as some sort of entity that governs over everything ~ not that He is completely in control but He provides an overriding sense of order. I find the less I try to control things, the more they work out the way they should. So I have a certain amount of faith in this greater order.

But when things get tough, I do find myself turning to some God-like being. I've never felt a dialogue between God and myself, though. It's more like me sending messages of wanting, sometimes in a whiny way.

So perhaps you would use the number initially to ask for something?

Yeah...If I had this number when I was younger, I know I would have seen it as a genie's lamp that grants a certain amount of wishes or questions. But I'm sure it would have been: "Be careful what you ask for." I might have wanted God to make this guy fall in love with me and then it would turn out to be a very destructive relationship. I would regret it later. I think God would realize that these were just whimsical, self-centered wishes and the gifts would be cut off if I had called Him or Her from that frame of mind.

I do feel that I have been taken care of by God in a lot of ways. As I've gotten older, I feel like my life is more in sync with whatever this power is that we call God. If I were to have God's phone number in this more mature frame of mind, I might want to call to thank Him or Her for all my good fortune.

I'm not so sure I'd want to get into a philosophical discussion with Him. But if God were willing to talk, there are many things I'd like to ask about.

What would you want to know?

I'd want to know about disease. I'm going into medicine, and it concerns me that viruses are going to snuff us out. Viruses are the one thing we have not been able to combat. Is our time limited on Earth because of the powers of viruses and, if so, is Earth going to go on without us?

What do you think God might say back to you?

I suppose if God were to respond, He or She might say: "Humans can't comprehend this broad thinking...You're just one stage in a whole continuum of life. There have been different forms of sophisticated life that lasted far longer than you have so far."

I do wonder if there are beings like us elsewhere. I just took this course on evolution, and it's overwhelming to think about all the time and space and whatever else may be out there in the universe. I'd love to talk to God about that.

Many people believe that there are aliens from other planets who have visited here. I just can't get myself to believe that. I really feel like we are so alone, but I'd like to know if this is true.

And does this God I'm talking about just govern Earth or all of the planets? What really is His or Her domain? When I start thinking about how far-reaching it could be, when all I know is this square corner, it starts to get overwhelming. I don't trip myself out thinking about this every day of course. [Laughs]

Hmmm... Okay. Back to this number, is there anything else that comes to mind that you might want to use it for?

I could ask for miracles such as finding homes and jobs for all the homeless people. Or for God to make the ground fertile in a country that has mostly desert and no food.

But mostly I would be interested in general understanding. I want to understand the world and God better. I am still afraid of asking too many questions and using up my genie bottle quota, though.

If I could have unlimited questions, one dominant one is: Do humans have an inherent defect? We are destroying the environment. Women are continually striving for equality. We continue to get into war. One group is always putting another group down. Is our short-sightedness a self-destruct button?

What do you think God's response might be?

I think God's answer could be something like: "That's your doing. I gave you a brain and the abilities to use it, and you're using it to selfish ends." That's partly why I'd be afraid to ask God too much because I'm afraid He'd say that we do have a defect. Hearing something like this from God would be very unsettling.

I do wonder if we are some experiment and the Earth is going to survive beyond us to try other experiments. Or are we on the path to something else? Is this completely random? Are we really reaching the point of some Armageddon and, if so, what is the fate of the human race?

My real concern is ~ if our current trends are all random ~ that nobody would answer this phone. [Laughs] If this were all just an evolutionary accident, then there is no one in charge. [Laughs]

More seriously, I've had dreams where I'm trying to call out on the phone and I can't get through. I keep misdialing and having to redial out, and it's always busy. It's a total anxiety nightmare. I may truly be afraid to call God's number for fear that nobody would answer. I'm not sure I want to learn that this is all an evolutionary accident.

Well, for the sake of this conversation, let's assume that Someone does answer.

Well, I don't believe it is an evolutionary accident. I would make the phone call. But one thing is for sure, I wouldn't ask about what will happen with my life. I'd be too afraid to know. Suppose I couldn't do anything about it.

I guess I could ask about earlier times in my life. I know I was probably too reliant on others' advice and direction at times. I imagine God would counsel me: "Don't be afraid of confusion. Don't be afraid of the chaos when you feel like you don't know where to go. There are many ways to live a full life without having to achieve in the way you think you have to."

It sounds like you've gone through times of confusion and doubts about your achievements.

My brother was a Phi Beta Kappa and graduated magna cum laude from Yale and I feel like a failure next to him. I could have graduated with honors from college, but I had a bad advisor and he did not push me to write a thesis as I could have. I really feel I could have done better. I guess I would want God to tell me, "It's okay what you have done."

The structured ways of academic honors and getting into this school or that ~ all that competitiveness gets me very anxious. I feel like I don't know another way so I want to achieve in that structure. Is there another way?

What do you think God might say about this?

I really wish I knew what God would say. It's hard for me to separate what I think from what God would think. If I truly knew what God would think, I wouldn't ask Him or Her. [Laughs]

Good point. Sarah, can you tell me a little about your religious background?

Well, I've never really gotten involved in organized religion. When I was a kid, my family would go to synagogue only on high holidays and get together during Seder with family or friends. I went to a very untraditional Hebrew school for about two years and then I had a bat mitzvah, but it was a social event more than anything else. I never really felt that connected to Judaism as a way of life although I do consider myself Jewish.

In college I took a course studying the New Testament with a great religion professor. We studied the biblical stories and looked at them from a historical context. It was very interesting. I was taught as a child that these biblical stories are similar to fables or myths and they did not really happen.

But there was so much written about the figure of Jesus. I do wonder if Jesus really existed. My professor said there probably was a historical Jesus. But who was he? I would ask God this. How much of what is in the Bible is the truth? I can't believe that any of it is more than a story. Although it did seem to take on a life of its own ~ being the story of Mark, then Luke and Matthew. The only thing we heard about Jesus while we were growing up was that he was Jewish.

That's an interesting question. Is there anything else you would like to ask?

I do wonder about psychic people. Do they really know something that the rest of us don't? My rational side wants to believe that tarot cards just work by coincidence. On the other hand, I don't want to discount the power of psychics.

I could ask God if there are people who have a more direct connection to Him or Her or the general electricity of the universe ~ or the general cosmic order. Can they truly tell us something beyond what we can see in our subjective day-to-day lives?

Have you ever used a psychic?

I've never been tempted to pay for a psychic. I know myself better than someone on a phone line. I would rather tune into my own inner voice for answers. When I need to make a decision about doing something, words sometimes come into my head: "Don't do that. Do this..." If I ignore this inner voice, I regret it. I'd like to ask God where that's coming from and how I can tune into that better. "Is it coming from You?"

I think God might tell me that I should absolutely listen to that voice and take as much time as I need to slow down and listen to it.

Hmmm...Anything else?

Well, yes. I'd want to ask God about death. Death scares me and I wrestle with not wanting to age or decay. I yearn to live perpetually in this organic world, which is impossible since we have organisms such as viruses that we succumb to. [Laughs]

My grandfather is dying right now. He has cancer of the bladder, and I would want to ask God: "Is this how you mean for him to go?" He is so healthy in other ways and not ready to go. I would want to ask God to spare my grandfather's life at this point in time.

But I do believe that there is a greater order. I'd be concerned that if I were to ask God to heal my grandfather, it might disrupt something else and something worse could happen. That's scary to think about. I would have to believe that God would not grant me that wish if it had such an impact.

That's an interesting thought. You think there may be a greater order that God has planned and if you used this

number to ask for a change, it might throw off other parts of His larger order?

Sometimes I think that, especially when I'm feeling insecure about making a decision and am afraid that if I don't choose the right one, everything is going to be disrupted. In my less neurotic moments I feel there is more flexibility and there is a general order instead of just one way. It depends on my mood and how in tune I am with how I really feel.

But what really happens after death? If we knew, would that change the way we approach our lives?

What do you think God might say back?

To this I think God would say, "It's all a continuum. Don't be so concerned with what happens after death, because you're here now."

✦

Sarah Dorn raised some interesting questions that I have pondered before. As an environmentalist, I have given great thought to why our dominant world culture is so destructive and so short term in our decisions about the environment, although I have never gone so far as to think that we have an inherent defect. I tend to believe that we've gone off course, perhaps led by negative forces within us. But I hold out hope that we will be able to learn in time to shift our practices and use more wisdom in our decision making about technology and the environment.

Sarah's questions about whether she was achieving in that structure in the right way deeply resonated within me. I grew up in a very conservative Ivy League family where not only my father but three of my siblings went to Yale. I instead went to a small liberal arts college in the boondocks of New York and was labeled an underachiever. When I finished college, I spent several years working in the National Park system in the west. My pattern for several years was to come back to my parents' home for visits and then head to the next job and adventure.

Once when I was back in Baltimore, my cousin asked me when I was going to get a real job. I was rather insecure at the time and took her words to heart and decided to move back to Baltimore to find a career. Needless to say, I was depressed for a solid two years as I tried to force my life and interests into the square box that I thought I was supposed to fit into. Over time I have learned that I'm just weird ~ in a good way ~ and even though I may move to the sound of a different drummer (my brother once asked me in all seriousness what planet I was from!), there is an overall purpose and direction that my life has taken. And that is okay. I actually have been able to find a community of friends who are similar to me, and this has helped me heal the insecurities about my weirdness.

But most of us are born and raised with powerful conditioning that tells us how to live and what to do to conform. It is amazing the thoughts I have in my head, to this day, of what a person from my background should and should not do. For example, I never call into any radio show to win a prize. Somehow I got it into my head that people from my social class do not do that even though I am certain no one told me that directly. Or I should not go out shopping without looking nice in proper clothes. I got over that one long ago and have no qualms about going to the grocery store in sweat pants now.

I'm convinced that the box that society tries to fit us into all the time does not work for everyone. But many of us try desperately to fit anyway and hence suffer all sorts of emotional malaise about it. I'm only glad that I've learned to be at peace with how different I am and no longer swirl in the depths of malaise these days ~ although it has taken most of my adult life to reach this place.

I love the way that Sarah finished the interview. A powerful concept that she reminded me of is the spiritual discipline of Be Here Now. Ram Dass wrote a best-selling book in 1971 with that title. The gist of it is that we can find spiritual wholeness if we just focus on the moment and drop our fears about the future and judgments about the past. This practice continually surfaces as a focus for my day-to-day life, especially when I am in the midst of very long-term projects that seem too daunting to complete.

There is some peace in thinking that we are all part of a continuum that God has planned and that our work is to maintain a sense of inner wholeness in the moment as we live our lives.

CHAPTER 7

GOD'S MASTER PLAN

KATHERINE CARTER
AGE: 85

GOD DOES NOT GIVE AN ANSWER TO ALL
OUR QUESTIONS, BUT, IN JESUS, GOD ENTERS
INTO THE HEART OF THE QUESTIONS.

~ LEONARDO BOFF

I have known Katherine Carter since I can remember. She was our housekeeper while I was growing up. When my brother and his wife bought my parents' house, she became their housekeeper. At age eighty-five, she's been going over to that same house to do ironing and laundry for more than thirty years.

I always loved to talk with Katherine. When I was young, I would hang out in the kitchen to be with her. She seemed so wise, and her life was so different from ours. At the end of every day she would get into her big, old station wagon and drive back to her all-black, middle-class community on the other side of Baltimore, a world so different from my all-white neighborhood.

Sometimes she would talk about her childhood on a farm in South Carolina. Or we would talk about other things. But I loved to hear her accent and the way she would drawl out my name with great warmth: "Mare-a-luv..."

When I started the book, I knew that I wanted to try to talk with Katherine. Her life had not been an easy one. She worked harder than anyone else I knew. She was also very devoted to her church.

So I called her up one day and asked her about being interviewed. She was very excited about the invitation. We arranged to do it one afternoon at her house. It was fall and she was in the throes of making jars and jars of green tomato relish when I arrived. She had an immense pot boiling on the stove that filled the room with a sweet vinegar aroma. I watched with awe as she efficiently ladled the green tomatoes and the liquid into Mason jars with her gnarled arthritic hands.

She quickly filled up the jars and then placed them into the hot water bath to seal. Then we moved to the living room where she removed some of the plastic sheets she keeps over her furniture to protect it from the chicken grease. Katherine was more shuffling than walking by this time. The arthritis in her knees was acting up. But she was still mobile. The room was full of pictures of her children and grandchildren, and it felt very cosy.

I set the tape recorder up on the coffee table and turned it on. As Katherine started talking, I looked at her. Here was a woman who had worked with her hands since she was young. And at eighty-five, she was still working. Her dark hands were thick and knobby in all the joints. She was wearing a faded cooking apron over a soft, blue cotton housedress with thin taupe knee-highs stretched over loose, flabby calves. Her gray hair was pulled back in a loose bun.

Katherine's warm eyes and furrowed, splotchy dark skin on her face broke into a deep smile as we started. She was enthralled that I had come to visit her for a book. Just months before, Katherine was recognized by her Baptist Church for fifty years of service to the congregation. She was happy to talk about God.

✧

If I gave you God's phone number, what would you do with it?

What would I do with God's phone number? I'd call Him on the phone. I'd talk to Him. There's a whole lot to talk with Him about and thank Him for. I'd thank Him for my life, my getting up in the morning all down through these years. For keeping me safe. For the angels that watch over me day and night. For my health and strength.

Would you have any particular things that you would want to talk with Him about?

There's nothing special I'd want to talk with Him about except maybe just to ask Him to take care of my children. I don't know about asking God any questions. We're not supposed to ask God about things. If something's happened, we're not supposed to question Him. He knows before we ask Him. He knows our uprisings, our downfalls. He knows every hair on our head. He's my Father and He's taken care of me. His guardian angels keep us from harm and danger. And He said that no evil will come near our dwelling place. He'd give his angels charge and nothing would happen to us.

So there is nothing that you would want to ask this great, wise being?

If something was going wrong maybe I'd ask Him for help. But if something was going right, you don't ask Him. You have to trust Him. I trust God every day.

[She starts reciting out loud.]

"They say the Lord is my shepherd. I shall not want. He maketh me to lie down in green pastures...Restores my soul; and leads me in the path of righteousness for His name's sake. Yea, though He walks through the valleys of the shadows of death...Fear no evil; for there with us, the rod and staff they comfort us. Prepare a table before us, in the presence of our enemy. He anoints our head with oil, our cup runs over. Surely goodness and mercy shall follow us all the days of our life. And we can dwell in the house of the Lord forever and ever... " [Psalm 23]

[Pause]

I wonder what you think Reverend King would say to this question. He carried God's plan out. Even though he was killed, he still carried the Lord's plan out. That's why we are as far as we are today, on account of King. That's right. He was killed, but he still had a reason.

Just like back in the Bible days, David did a lot of bad things, but he was still God's chosen son. Martin Luther King was doing God's work. He had a dream that he would get killed or something would happen to him and he carried God's dream out anyway. But he had another dream and that was that all children ~ all people ~ would be recognized in God. And they could sit down together. And eat together. Even down there in the South. He didn't care who they were so long as they could sit down and be together.

You know you weren't allowed to sit at the table with white folks. You weren't allowed to go into the bathroom. You weren't allowed to eat. You had to sit at the back of the bus. I used to have to sit at the back of the bus. I remember that. It wasn't anything like it is today.

Would you want to ask God why it is that someone like Martin Luther King had to do His work?

I wouldn't ask God because He knows that He had a plan for Reverend King's life. We all have a plan. God has a plan for all of our lives, a plan every day. You've got to do

God's will, not your will. People are always doing their will.

Now, Mare, you think you've got a plan for your life. But God's got a plan for you. He's got a plan for you to get married when you're supposed to. That's right. When He gets the right one for you, you'll get it. Just like your brother, Joe. I don't care how many girlfriends he had, he hasn't married yet. God has a plan for him, too.

When I was younger and working in the cotton and corn fields, that was part of God's plan. We had no other plan. We had no other way to make a living. We picked cotton all day long and hoed it and then we'd carry it to the gin where the seeds come out. We'd pull the shucks in the corn stalks and tie it up in bundles. We'd also cut sugar cane and pull the fodder off to make syrup out of the cane. My father would boil the syrup over the fire and stir it and stir it.

God's plan. God said that if you don't work then you have no bread. Some people don't understand that. That's right there in the Bible.

Some people don't work very hard. Is that God's plan?

No. They're lazy, no good. That's not God's plan. He means for us to work and make a living with the sweat of our eyebrows. He doesn't mean for us to go out and take it from somebody else. That's what some do.

I've been working ever since I was twelve years old. There were ten of us in my family, and we all worked in the cotton and corn fields. Then I came to Philadelphia to be with my uncle. I was about nineteen then, in 1929. I did not go to high school, though. I left school after fourth grade.

Do you think that was part of God's plan for you to not continue school?

Well, I don't know. But I wasn't able to go because I had

to work. But the Lord helped me learn how to write and count. Now look at me right here with my own house. My husband and I got the money to buy this house in 1953.

We don't understand how we get where we got. It's just because God wanted it that way. When God wants you to have something, you have it. Nobody can take it away from you. When God doesn't want you to have it, then you don't get it. A Master Plan.

When my son went to school, we couldn't get new shoes for his feet. When he didn't have any soles left on his shoes, we pasted boards on the bottom of them. That's what he wore.

My son went to high school, and the Lord fixed it so he won a scholarship and went to Morgan State. And then in the army, he went to medical school. He's a doctor now. He always wanted to be one. I had no money to send him to college, but the Lord made a way. He sent him. Now he's a retired colonel. The Lord's been good to me.

Now my husband is up there in Heaven.

Katherine, if you could call Heaven and your husband is up there, would you like to talk to him?

No. I know someday I'll be up there and I'll meet him up there. If not, it'll be a different story. We'll just hope for the best. That's right, all part of the Master's Plan.

Many people have gone on. I'm still here. There must be a reason for me to stay here. My sister is younger than I am. She can hardly walk. She's got this inner ear thing, so she has to walk with a cane. But I can still walk.

I just thank God every day because I can work and do for myself. I still clean house for other people. I have a lot to be thankful for. Some who are seventy-five can't do what I do. I can wash and iron. I cut grass. I still work in my garden out there.

Tell me, when you were little, did you go to church?

Every Sunday. We went to Sunday school and church at the Mt. Level Baptist Church in Ayden, North Carolina. We walked a couple miles to get there. There wasn't any horse and buggy wagon for us. All my life I've been a Baptist. My grandmother, my great-grandmother, they all were Baptist.

There's not too much else to say. I'd just thank Him for what He did for me all down through these years. Kept me from harm and danger. Thank God.

✧

I had to chuckle a little when Katherine told me that God has a plan for me to find a husband. Whenever I would see her after a lapse of several years, the first question she would always ask me was whether I had found a husband yet. It was not important to her where I was living or what type of work I was doing. Katherine was very traditional and believed that the only way to fulfill your life was if you had found a husband or wife.

A part of me bristled at Katherine's question, though. Her traditional views offended my highly developed feminist values. If Katherine did not ask it with such warmth in her voice, I know my responses would have been more curt. I had worked internationally, headed a nonprofit organization, bought and sold a house ~ all rungs of accomplishment for any professional. Yet my life was still not complete in her eyes. Deep down I knew she was right. My personal life did have a void. While I was searching quietly and deliberately for that elusive soul mate, I still came home only to my cats, and no one held me tight in my bed and shared their joys and troubles with me at night.

It was very hard for me to see my two younger sisters marry before me. Sitting through their ceremonies brought up that familiar inner carping: "There must be something wrong with me since I'm still single and they've found their life mates." When one of my sisters had her first child, a surging emptiness tore through me even more deeply. I yearned to know why love came so easily to others and not me. I could acknowledge this pain only to myself and my closest friends. To the rest of the world, I tried to put on the career woman persona for them to see. And Katherine always cut right through that in her direct way to remind me of this vacuum. At least she always asked it with her rough love.

I was fascinated with how faithfully Katherine believed in God's plan. I think she really believed that God coordinates our day-to-day activities. I don't think our lives are as closely orchestrated by God as Katherine believes. But I feel a tinge of envy that she gives so much control over to Him. I take more personal responsibility for my decisions on a mundane level, and this adds a certain level of stress. I think her life may be somewhat easier for this.

I have long grappled with the concept of some universal wisdom that lays out our life plan. Perhaps, before we are born, our souls come to agreement with the Universe/God on the work that we are meant to do in that lifetime. Many people believe that we choose our parents before we are born, and I agree with this. I would take it further and add that we quite possibly choose our life work while we are still souls waiting to reincarnate. These choices are ones that can further us on our spiritual journey as souls reaching a higher level of evolution.

When I was leaving Ann Arbor in 1994, I had my heart set on moving to the Pacific Northwest. I was drawn to the strong environmentally conscious focus there. I even flew out and found a house to rent.

Six weeks before I was to leave, my job sent me on a two-week consulting trip to the Caribbean. For some inexplicable reason while I was down there, I started crying every night. I had no idea what was going on. When I flew out the last morning and gazed out the window as the plane circled over the turquoise Caribbean waters, everything inside me said that I needed to come back to this region and there was no way that I could move to the Northwest. So I canceled my plans to move to Washington State.

The only thing guiding my decisions during that time of extreme confusion were my instincts. When I returned from the Caribbean, my inner voice was veritably yelling to me that I was not to move to Washington State. I had to halt all of my plans and make alternative plans in a dark time of personal chaos. I ended up storing my belongings in my parents' basement and eventually settling back into Baltimore. There was no logic to my doing this from a practical standpoint.

What I have come to realize was that I was meant to come back to the Mid-Atlantic to really heal my relationship with my family and continue on my spiritual journey here. There was work that I needed to do in the Baltimore-Washington region.

I still don't understand what it was that opened up in me that made me so emotional in the midst of the consulting trip. But I have come to trust that, whatever it was, it helped steer me toward what I now believe is my true path of growth and spiritual learning ~ a path that my soul may well have agreed to before I was even born.

There is another side to this, however. I believe that many people do not live up to their plan. They get paralyzed by fear, and it blocks them from achieving their potential. Katherine so simply stated: "When God wants you to have something, you have it. Nobody can take it away from you." Actually I think it is quite easy for us to personally take it away from ourselves. Through alcohol or other types of addiction or fears, we can succumb to mediocrity and never develop into the fullest extent of who we could be.

Marianne Williamson wrote and Nelson Mandela quoted in his inauguration speech:

Our deepest fear is not that we are inadequate.
Our deepest fear is that we are powerful beyond measure.
It is our light, not our darkness, that most frightens us.
We ask ourselves, Who am I to be brilliant, gorgeous,
talented, fabulous?
Actually, who are you not to be? You are a child of God.
Your playing small does not serve the world.
There's nothing enlightened about shrinking so that
other people won't feel insecure around you.
We are all meant to shine, as children do.
We were born to make manifest the glory of God that is
within us.
It's not just some of us; it's in everyone.
As we let our own light shine, we unconsciously give
other people permission to do the same.
As we are liberated from our own fear,
our presence automatically liberates others.

There are many people who are frightened by their own light and consequently are limiting themselves to playing small. I have tried to move through my fears to "shine" by forming my own education/consulting company and leading workshops on environmental topics, but I know these are simply the present mountains to climb. I am sure that there are more ahead.

I can't help but believe that those who play small disappoint God, and these people will return in another lifetime to try again to learn to recognize and walk in the fullness of their inner light. My struggle in this lifetime is to continue to recognize it in myself.

CHAPTER 8

PROVE IT

SCOTT WILLEMSEN*
AGE: 28

IF YOU DON'T FEEL CLOSE TO GOD,
GUESS WHO HAS MOVED?

~ CHURCH POSTER

I have some good friends outside Newark, New Jersey, who organize a Groundhog's Day party in the middle of winter each year. It's a very silly event based on all the hoopla about how long winter will be, according to a groundhog in Pennsylvania who does or does not see his shadow when he emerges from his hole. Since I was living closer to these friends for the first time in years, I was eager to attend their annual event.

My friends were both involved in counseling at-risk youth; thus, most of the people at the party were in similar fields. Early on in the party, I was drawn to one particular man there named Scott Willemsen. With his curly blonde hair and strong build, Scott had an easy, confident way about him. As the night wore on, I could see that I was not alone; Scott's charisma attracted numerous women throughout the entire party.

Scott and I were introduced and, as is the norm, we

---

*not his real name

talked about our work ~ he trained youth in woodworking skills and I did assorted other part-time work while working on the book. Scott spoke very articulately and struck me as a natural leader. I was intrigued by him, so I invited him to consider being interviewed. He said, "Sure."

Scott's weekend was very tight, so the only time he could schedule the interview was Monday right after he finished work. Thus I made arrangements to extend my stay and meet him at the training center late Monday afternoon.

The center was in an industrial part of Newark, and it was a bit harrowing driving through the surrounding run-down neighborhoods, but I finally found it. By the time I got there, the students had left for the day, and the smell of fresh-sawn wood hung in the cavernous wood shop area inside the building. We held the interview in a small classroom off to one side. Scott's heavy khaki pants and work boots were covered with sawdust. I could see that he was physically tired, but his thoughts were clear as he spoke.

✧

If I gave you God's phone number, what would you do with it?

What if you don't believe that there is a being who would answer that number?

Well, then I suppose you are in this dilemma of being given a phone number.

I don't believe in God, and therefore I don't believe that someone could give me such a number.

Well...suppose I said I really had it and did give it to you?

It would be impossible. I would think it was a joke. If you tried to give me a phone number to God, I'd have to accept that He existed. Or It. Whatever you want to call It. But I don't believe in God.

There's a difference between asking God questions and just having things I've questioned. There are things I question, of course.

So you do have questions...

Oh, yeah, I have lots of questions such as: "Where did we come from?" Or: "What's the universe?" But I don't need to believe that somebody created all of this or that there's somebody out there in control of it. Many people need to have those questions answered, but I don't need that for my soul.

I just don't think of an entity creating everything like some religious people do. They say God created the first primate. I don't believe that. I think the theory of evolution is very plausible.

I like the idea of mind-blowing questions such as: "What's out there?" My guess is that there are a lot of other things out there just like we're experiencing here. It's a difficult question. You can try to answer it, but you hit a certain point where you just go in circles. If you want to have an answer, then you can put God there.

For most people, that's what God's there for. But I don't feel like I need an answer to some of those questions. I think I'll know it when I have the answer.

Do you think there may be a time when you might have some of these answers?

Maybe upon death. That's the only time I could imagine clarity. Unless I'm lucky enough to have some sort of clarifying experience in my lifetime. Some people discover religion, and that gives them an explanation that suits them. But I can't forecast whether that will happen to me. But if it does ~ wonderful! If it doesn't ~ wonderful also. I don't feel the need to have religion, even though I was brought up in one.

How do you define religion?

I consider religion a vehicle. Just about every religion has a common basis for evolution, a God, a prophet, a virgin mother of some sort. I think there are regional and cultural differences in them, but they all do the same thing, which is provide an explanation or a context for answering why we are here.

I satisfy my need to answer "Why are we here?" by learning about as many scientific or philosophical explanations as I can. To me the interesting part is just the thinking about it. In science, you keep looking for the answers.

I'm not suggesting that everything has a scientific answer. I think religious people have reasons for things that are non-scientific based on God. That's fine, but there is no basis for their reasons. Look at the Bible. Many people believe in the miracles talked about in the Bible. But these miracles happened only once.

When a scientific statement is made, there has to be some empirical evidence to support it. When you do something over and over again, you can deduce it's going to happen again. That makes a lot of sense to me. It's not based on faith or anything else. Certainly there are things that science can't answer. Then we just need to keep searching for those answers.

Does science become a kind of religion?

Is science a religion? It could be, but I don't think so. Maybe it's two different things. Science for the things that could be answered and religion for those that can't be answered. Many famous scientists were very spiritual. Einstein grew much more spiritual as his career evolved, as he got further and further into many of these questions. Newton was very religious and yet extremely mathematical. Perhaps there is some association between religion and science, but I don't see it.

But suppose I truly gave you a phone number...

If you gave me a phone number, I think I would know whether this was God's number or not. I would feel it. Or, if I called the number, I would know whether it was God on the other end. There would have to be that kind of proof.

And if some entity that called itself God answered, I would tell It, "Give me proof! Perform a miracle!" [Laughing]

People of certain faiths would never question their God. I would. You'd be a fool not to.

Suppose a miracle did happen in front of you?

[Pause]

I'd be amazed.

I don't know. This would mean that I would have to believe in God. I'm trying to avoid the premise that God exists. It is difficult for me to consider any miracle because then I start getting into a place where God might exist. And that's not the question. The question is if you had God's number. I don't believe God exists. [Laughs]

When I am asked about God's phone number, it makes me wonder: "Well, why don't I believe in God?" I feel fine about not believing in God. It's not something that I'm upset about or terribly proud about. It's neither. I'm just ambivalent.

I do think about the question of God often because science can take you only so far. After that you have to wonder: "What's next?" And personally, it blows me away. But it doesn't make me feel insecure ~ not being able to have an answer for it.

Truthfully, religion hasn't played a very impressive role in history. Most of the things I've read about religion over the years are more derogatory, more culture stamping than anything else.

Let me ask you this...Have there ever been times in your life when you might have been really struggling and you needed clarity and you wanted to ask something greater than yourself for answers?

Certainly there have been times when I have wanted more clarity in my life, and it manifested in confusion and anxiety. But I never looked up to the clouds and said, "Oh, why is this happening to me?" I always looked for answers through the confusion. But it was never... [Long pause] ...through God.

I didn't really grow up believing in God although I suppose I grew up in a religious setting. I went to a Lutheran Church but never really bought into it. Lutherans can be pretty guilt-trippy. But I never felt fear. I was never God fearing or felt guilty even when I stopped going.

I never really understood why I was in church. My parents just took us. Their parents took them to church, so they took us. It was just a repeating cycle like with a lot of families.

It was never: "You have the option of going to church." That is what it should have been. I think that if you're going to take your kids to church, don't take them to just one. Take them to all of them, and let them choose which one they like the best. At least don't take them to a specific church until they're ready to make that decision. Educate them first.

But that is not what my parents did. I went to church and was confirmed and went through those hoops until I was about fifteen. Then I really started putting on the heat and being rebellious.

Yeah, that's when most of us got rebellious.

But my feelings about church didn't really hit me until my early twenties. It was at my grandfather's funeral. The pastor was reading the Apostle's Creed or something like that and I knew the words by rote. Up until that point, I hadn't really listened to the words: "I believe in the Father, the Son and the Holy Ghost, the community of Saints, the forgiveness of sin..." It hit me, "I don't believe in this. Why am I saying it?" A lot of it angered me.

I was also angered to hear this person say that my grandfather was taken away for a reason. My grandfather had Alzheimer's disease and died of it. It was that straightforward. If there is a God to give him Alzheimer's disease to take him away, then there's something wrong with that God. That was really the final straw.

If there is a God and that is It's way of handling things, then I'm not going to believe in It. It just seems too easy to have an explanation that involves God for everything. "God's will." You could say that about anything. That's too unsettling for me.

I think people die because their bodies just give out. We're not the only organisms around. There are viruses and bacteria and all kinds of things that live and die. Sometimes we die with them. I'm not a "humanocentric" person. Not enough credit is given to other organisms.

We're just another organism that happens to have done a better job manipulating our natural environment and our elements. We've made some positive things like alloys or metal. Creating a desk or a chair takes a heck of a lot of cerebral work. We're the only animals that ~ so far as we know ~ have been able to do this as we have on this planet. It has probably happened on other planets.

Hmmm...Do you think we have a soul?

I do think every living organism has a soul. At least larger organisms, not necessarily viruses and bacteria. I think it takes a combination of things such as having consciousness and the ability to reason to have a soul. A dog might have a soul. Or a horse or cow might have one, too.

I don't think the soul dies when a person dies. It may possibly take the form of energy. Maybe it's recycled. That might not be a bad thing. Maybe there is a part of the soul that is energy and goes back out to be reabsorbed. It's just speculation, but if it is energy, there must be a source somewhere. Must be some mass of it. I'm not so scientific that I believe that when you die, you just expire and that's it.

This may be getting way off topic, but I had an out-of-body experience once. It was really incredible, but there was nothing religious about it. It was just a physical experience.

I was lying in bed not yet asleep. All of a sudden I felt very clear. It felt as if I had shifted to another kind of consciousness. I was lying on my back, very alert and very conscious. I couldn't move a muscle in my body. I couldn't see anything. It was as if my senses were turned off. Yet I was conscious ~ very awake. It was very frightening.

Then I felt as if I were being separated from my body. My awareness shifted to being above my head, and I could feel the presence of my body underneath me. I lifted and drifted down to the end of the bed and did this lateral movement, and then I was looking back at my own feet.

Then it just reversed, and I switched back and dropped back into my body. As soon as I dropped back down, I could move. I was conscious throughout the whole process.

That's amazing.

I could see my girlfriend when it happened. [Laughing] I could see my feet and my body underneath the sheets. I could see her next to me, and that was the only point when I felt unafraid. In the moment, I thought I must have been scaring the shit out of her. I had no perception of what my face was doing. I just knew something was happening, and the only way I could try to explain it was from my past experiences of doing something physical. But this was very different. It was my soul, perhaps. It was something else.

Of course I did a heck of a lot of reading about it afterward. It seems a lot of people have had the same experience with the same description, and they call it astral projection. I only wish it would happen again. [Laughs] But throughout that whole time, I never once considered religion or God as an explanation.

I believe there is a soul or another dimension to us that we're not sensitive to. It can manifest itself in ghost sightings or people having out-of-body experiences or telekinesis or being able to read somebody's mind. We don't have the scientific parameters to define it or understand it or put it into a context so that everybody can read or feel or know it. But just because we don't have those parameters doesn't mean these phenomena don't exist.

So this is one of those areas where you are comfortable with the unknowns ~ the unanswered questions?

Yes, I'm comfortable with not knowing. I don't feel that

I need to give somebody like God credit for it.

✦

Scott was such a strong, secure person that I suppose that he did not need spirituality in his life ~ so far. He prompted me to remember a friend whom I knew when he was in his late thirties. My friend, James, was a deeply spiritual man who meditated a great deal. He shared with me that he was not spiritual at all in his twenties but was quite the lady's man and had many lovers. But after he married and his wife left him for another man, he became severely depressed and sought out meditation. This practice was what helped him find answers and some peace in his heart. James was still very wounded when I met him, however. I wondered if Scott's inner strength and lack of a need for God would be tested in the future, too.

Scott was still young, and he had already had an out-of-body experience. It struck me that he might be destined for more inexplicable experiences that would lead him to finding God. I do doubt that Scott will go to his grave with the same beliefs that he had as a twenty-eight-year-old. Of course, I am biased, too. I know that I would like him to be open in time to the concept of a phone number to God.

His out-of-body experience was fascinating to listen to. I have never experienced that nor have I spoken with too many people who have. But Scott was such a secure person within himself. It made me wonder if the reason that he had this metaphysical incident was that his spirit body was strong enough to allow him to have it. My sense is that people who have such experiences are only those strong and stable enough to integrate it.

I felt a kind of strange admiration for Scott that he could live with all the unanswered questions. I guess I am one of those people who feels better with an answer. It makes so much sense for me to consider phenomena such as out-of-body experiences as one more manifestation of there being a spirit world beyond the physical world and God being the Creator of it all.

Overall, I really felt that Scott's perception of religion as a vehicle only looked at the surface of what the spiritual part of religion offers. He believed that religion was all about answering questions. He's never even considered, much less experienced, the deeper aspects of a spiritual life. Yet those who really delve into profound spiritual experiences know of the love that we can feel from God. I'm talking about the depth of bliss you experience when you know you're connected with God and in that moment you feel your heart bursting with a spiritual love, not the kind of love you have toward a lover.

There have been moments when I have sat in front of my altar and lit the candle to sit in the stillness of that space, and a deep peace framed by joy seeped into me. It was a feeling of powerful warmth sinking into the center of my chest. I even experienced this once in the dentist's chair, of all places. What prompted it were the leaves of a maple tree up close to the large window there. The office is on the fourth floor, and squirrels sitting in the maple tree are on an eye level with those looking out the window. One day I was waiting for the dentist to come in to talk with me, and I was mesmerized by the leaves. They began to take on a golden hue as if the entire tree were emanating a soft glow. In that instant, I felt so connected to the tree and its leaves and deeply sensed the life force within it. God was that tree in that moment.

The times that I have experienced this bliss make me believe that I'm touching a piece of what many consider Heaven to be. And Heaven is actually something that we can experience here on Earth as opposed to the Christian belief that we need to wait until after we die to find it.

CHAPTER 9

SHOT OUT OF MY SHOES

MARY THOMAS*
AGE: 61

THE GLORY OF GOD WILL BE REVEALED,
AND ALL PEOPLE WILL SEE IT.
THE LORD HIMSELF HAS PROMISED THIS.

~ ISAIAH 40:5

As a child, I spent most of my free time over at my cousins' house and would often see their housekeeper, Mary Thomas, at work. Mary was constantly shooing us out off the first floor and sending us outside to play. I suppose she was in her forties at the time.

Shortly after I started the book, my aunt invited me over for lunch, and I was surprised to find Mary there. She still came over to dust and clean one day a week. It had been twenty years since I'd seen her, but she still attacked the dirt with the same vengeance. She was wearing the same cotton button-up shirt over polyester pants with plain white canvas sneakers. Her hair was grayer than I remembered, but it was still mostly dark and thick and styled around her face.

Mary remembered me and we caught up a little. The sternness that I remembered as a child had waned to a shy, friendly warmth as she recognized that I was now an adult

---

*not her real name

83

with my own life. She wanted to hear what work I was doing and whether I was married yet. I told her a little about the book and that I was still single and that was okay.

After I described my book to Mary, she seemed quite interested in it. She shared that she was very active in her church and then in a very shy voice asked whether she could be interviewed. I could not ~ nor did I want to ~ say "no" to her. I had not talked with many people as religious as Mary was.

My aunt was delighted that she could play a small role in linking me with another person for my book, so she offered her house for the interview. Thus we set it for the following week.

The next week I returned to my aunt's house at the appointed time. Mary was just putting the cleaning supplies away and had this look of excitement as if she were being asked to meet the President. Once she put everything away, she announced that she was ready. We sat down on the broad couch in the den, whereupon she pulled out a folded piece of paper. I was a little taken aback at this. It appeared she had done some homework for the interview. No one else had come prepared for an interview like this. I encouraged her to read what she had written.

✧

If I gave you God's phone number, what would you do with it?

Mare, I've put down a few notes after I talked with you, and this is what came to me.

[She picks up her paper and starts to read.]

I would dial the number and get Him on the phone. When He picked up the phone, I would tell Him who I was. Then I would tell Him how much I loved Him. I would thank and praise Him for all His goodness and mercies that He had bestowed upon me. I would glorify and worship His name because His name is the greatest of all names, a name that is given above every name. For at the name of Jesus, every knee should bow of things in Earth and things under the Earth, that every tongue should confess that Jesus Christ is Lord to the glory of God the Father.

Next, I would thank Him for dying on the cruel cross and giving me new life, hope and eternal life and that I can have it more abundantly. I found that in St. John 10:10.

Following that, I would thank and praise Him for blessing me with His precious Holy Ghost, which He has placed inside of me and sealed me to the day of redemption and allowed me to speak in other tongues as the Spirit has given me the utterance just like the Scripture has said in Acts 2:4.

Then I would thank and praise Him for His guidance as He has left His word for me to live by and direct my path. For as Peter wrote in Acts 2:38, we must repent and be baptized in the name of Jesus Christ for the remission of sins, and ye shall receive the gift of the Holy Ghost. I found out that when we repent, we have to make a complete turn in our lives and have it broken in a contrite spirit for these things God will not despise. I found that in Psalms 51:17.

To be baptized is to immerse in water, for Jesus was immersed in the river of Jordan. Remission of sin is that Jesus came to pardon us of our sins. Of this we should be thankful.

Come, let us think about this. Here is a man who is willing to forgive us for sinning against Him, and that's not all. He is willing to give us a free gift. All we have to do is to believe and take it. We need to follow His directions in the greatest book in the world, the Bible, and it's yours. I have found that if you follow the Book of Acts, you will come out all right. For what a mighty God He is.

Well, at this point I want to thank Him for this great

honor that He has clothed me with so that I can tell others about God's goodness and mercies and how He will forgive us of our sins and remember them no more. To me, this is awesome. We as a people could never do this for we hold all sorts of evil against each other. Some we will forgive, and some we never forget or forgive. What a mighty God we serve here.

Oh, by the way, others would have to know about this great God that I have just got finished talking to. For you know we are God's witnesses, and the only way that others can know about this man, Jesus, is through us that know so much about Him.

He can talk to us through His word. We can pray to Him at any hour of the day or night. Shedding tears is not a crime ~ all we need to do is be willing to humble ourselves and pray out of the depths of our hearts. For the Scripture also says: "Out of the heart comes the issues of life."

In other words, whatever you set your heart to, it says who you are (your identity). He will help you through your many trials, sufferings and afflictions. He will have mercy on each and every one of us. He can and will heal our bodies and our minds, but we must believe that He can and will do these things for us.

Now maybe a question comes into your mind. How do you know that He will do all these things? Well, when we read about His crucifixion, we know that He tasted sin for every man because He loved us so much. And you find that in Matthew 27.

I must come to a close now but before I do, I would like to let you know that no man on this Earth has been able to do the things for me that God has done. He has given me peace in the midst of many storms that came up in my life. I want to encourage anyone to try the Man, and I promise you that He will never leave you nor forsake you. Read His Word and ask Him to open up your understanding, and guess what? He will.

Now, Mare, I truly hope that you can get something out of this which I have placed on this paper. Nevertheless, this comes from my heart, and one thing you can look forward to is that there is always another chapter to this thing. It never runs out. And of this I am truly grateful.

[And then she reads her name as if she had just read a letter out loud to me: "signed, Mary G. Thomas" and she puts down her papers.]

Well, this is most interesting to me. You wrote a treatise there. So one of the first things you would do is thank Him. Do you imagine that He would say anything back to you as you were thanking Him and praising him?

Well, I think He would be so glad that I was thanking Him that He would pour His spirit the more. The more you thank Him, the more He comes down to you and blesses your soul. When you give Him the highest praise, which is Hallelujah, this He glorifies because this is what He gave us our tongues for ~ to praise Him. He came that we would honor and respect Him. All He asks for is for respect just the same as you would respect your father and your mother.

But would you have any inclination to ask any questions? A lot of people might have questions for Him if they could talk to God directly.

Well, there probably are a lot of questions in many people's minds. They might want to know why God allowed certain situations to happen to them. I think a lot of people might have questions in their minds and in their hearts about the things that are going on these days. Knowing that there is One that is greater above us might help them.

Would you have any questions yourself?

Well, [she whispers] I didn't mean to talk about this...But when I first got Him in my life, I was wondering why He would save such a person as I. I felt unworthy of His...His anointing or His spirit coming within me. But as I went on to know Him and began to learn how to pray and learn how to read His Word, I found out that it was just His love that He had for the whole world. He came not to condemn the world but to save those that were lost. And the whole world was lost.

I have learned that as you go on to know Him, your very thoughts change. If you look at the crucifixion of Jesus Christ, of all the things that he had to go through, you would wonder why would God do such as thing as this? He didn't have to do it. But He did it because He loved the world that He made, including the people that He put in it. God was trying to find someone on Earth that was worthy enough to take this assignment. But there was so much sin on the Earth at the time no one was worthy enough. So He had to give all He had, which was His son.

So you're saying that when you first found God, you wondered if you were worthy enough. But your questions would be very different right now?

Right. Because I've learned more about Him and how He operates. Christ tasted sin for every man. He loved the whole world, and this is why He suffered and He died. And it's His love that brought forth everything you see around us: the trees, the grass, all the birds, all the animals. He put love into action, and I believe that the reason why He had to do that was because a whole lot of people wouldn't have understood Him if He hadn't had something tangible to show you. All the animals and the trees ~ you can touch them.

I found that He uses things that you deal with every day

to show you who He is. He owns everything. So He may lead you to a four-leaf clover that represents His love and beauty. Then He'd bring a message to your mind about how that four-leaf clover is equal to Him. His love is beautiful, and everything He made was good. It wasn't bad. It wasn't corrupt. It was beautiful.

Do you think there is bad and good? Would you have any questions for God about that?

Oh, yes, there's bad and good in everything. I have to go back a little bit. It started in Eden. There in Genesis, God placed Adam and Eve in the beautiful garden and told them that they could touch all the trees but one, which was the Tree of Good and Knowledge. If you ever read the story, this serpent came to Eve and beguiled her. He told her that God didn't want them to know about this tree because they would become like Him. Then Eve went on and offered it to Adam, who forgot that God told them not to touch that Tree.

He didn't think, he didn't use his mind. This is where Satan or the Devil can get you ~ through your mind. If he gets your mind, he got you. And that's what he did to Adam and Eve. This is where God had to punish them. He gave Eve the pain of bearing children. And Adam had to work by the sweat of his brow. This is where natural death came forth. Because of their disobedience, the whole world has to suffer.

This is where pain and guilt and corruption came from. Satan was a beautiful angel and one of the main directors of music, but he fell. He got too big for himself, and this is why he had to be thrown out of Heaven. He had nerve enough to take God up on the mountain and show him all the beautiful things and say, "If You give me this, I will make You as incredible as all this beautiful stuff around you." But he was stupid because he didn't realize that God owned everything, and what could he give Him? God even owned Satan. [Laughing] But this is the way the mind can fool you.

Well, are there any other questions that you might pose to God or about any current issues, anything going on in the world today? Things that don't really make sense to you?

Well, a lot of it doesn't make sense, really, when I hear of all the murders, the senseless things that are happening. I don't believe that God is really doing it. I think it's man's mind that's fooling him and getting him to do all these crazy things. God never made all this evil. It's just because man has lost his spiritual side, and because of this, he's allowing Satan to use it.

Yet God says, "There is nothing under the sun that hasn't already been done." So that tells me that this has already been before. Remember all of the sin that was going on in the city of Sodom and Gomorrah? Evidently all these things that are going on now have happened before our time. People use a phrase now: What goes around, comes around. Just like that, I think all of these things have taken place before.

So it sounds like your conversation with God would be kind of short.

Well, I made it short today because as I was typing, I was saying to God, "Lord, she said about an hour." But I can't tell all this in one hour, because it's something that continuously goes on.

You pray a lot, don't you?

Yes, I do. The Scriptures say man should always pray. A lot of people think that your prayers are made up of special words. It's not like that. You can pray to God just like you're talking to me. He understands your groans and moans. He knows what you want to say to Him even before you say it. Yet He wants you to say it to Him. You can go to Him with all those secret things that you have hidden deep down that you probably don't want anybody else to know. And one thing I say is, all these secrets and deep things that we have within us, He will never tell anybody else. And that's what's so awesome about Him.

No, I can't imagine God gossiping. That's a really funny thought. (Laughing)

Right. That's true. That's one person we can trust and we won't have to hear it again, right? [More laughter]

You mentioned "speaking in tongues" in your piece that you wrote up. Do you speak in tongues?

Yes, I do. When I first got saved and baptized in the name of Jesus Christ, they told me that I had to tarry for the Holy Ghost. That means wait for the Holy Ghost. All of this is found in the Book of Acts. But while you're waiting, you pray and you start thanking Him.

So I went on and did as I was told. I began to thank God through praises, and that's when it came. I will never forget it. I was only nineteen. I was at the church altar, and different people were kneeling beside me and praising the Lord with me. They began to sing a song, and it was so beautiful. As they sang, I looked up into the stained window glass and was shocked to see a big light coming to me, and it looked like it was going to hit me in my chest. I just began to sing and praise the Lord. I began to thank God from the depths of my heart, and I don't remember anything else after that. When I came to, I was speaking in these tongues that the Lord had given me. It was in another language. Before I knew anything, they were putting my shoes on. I had shot out of my shoes! An older lady who was like the mother of the church said to me, "This is what we pray for."

They prayed for all of us who become saved to be able to speak in tongues. The next week after you got baptized, they would tell you to be at the church at such a time, and these praying women would meet you there and they would pray along with you in the church.

Mary, what exactly is speaking in tongues?

Speaking in tongues is talking to God directly. It's a very difficult thing that takes belief because it is nothing but the spirit of God that He has sealed you with to the day of redemption. Sometimes people give a message, but there must be an interpreter to interpret. God's going to have an interpreter in the midst to translate. It's not all the time that you're giving a message, though. You can praise Him through this speaking in tongues and glorify Him. You have to experience it. It's not something that I can just go "Pffft!" and go into.

It's just an awesome thing. It seems as though the more you get of God, the more you want of Him. He said, "He that hungers and thirsts after righteousness shall be filled." It runs over, it spills over and this is the way the Holy Ghost works.

It's all in the Book of Acts. I am asking you to please read it. It's for you and your children and your children's children. It's for the whole world. The Scripture is the greatest storybook ever been read. It never gets stale. There's always something to learn. It's always refreshing, even if you've read those same parts before.

Sometimes I wish I could just take it and put it on my hand and just put it in you to get you to see what I'm seeing and feel what I'm feeling. But I can't do that, you got to get it for yourself, come to the knowledge that you want yourself.

Do you ever feel like asking God about how can you bring more people to this?

Yes, yes. And God says you've got to get out there. You got to work for it. You got to tell the story, continuously tell the story until you've convinced them. I think the scripture says: "Command them to come." Whether they want to come or not, command them. Tell them to follow you. God wants your heart. This is the heart surgery that God wants to do to His people. Cast out the old one. Get them a new heart.

Mary, can you tell me how you first found God?

Well... [pause] ...I was raised by my grandparents and they went to a Methodist Church. We went with them and attended Sunday school. I remember we had to memorize little picture cards with verses every Sunday. We weren't allowed to do anything on Sundays except eat. No work.

But it was not fulfilling. It felt like there was a vacuum in me. I was in my late teens and had finished high school and gotten a housekeeping job. But there was still this vacuum.

Then my mother told me about this Apostolic Way. She took me to one of the services and said, "Well, I'm not going to tell you too much about it now. I'm just going to pray for you." And so she did. That's how I got into it. It changed my life. That's the reason I said in this paper, "No man on this Earth has been able to do the things that God has done for me. He gave me peace within myself." That's right.

How would you end this conversation with God on the phone?

Well, I don't know... [long pause] ...Maybe I would sing to Him. I love to sing and have taken lessons in it. I've been singing in my Apostolic Church choir every week for forty-six years. And God knows that I'll be talking to Him again very soon anyway.

✦

It was fascinating to hear Mary talk about speaking in tongues. I had heard people speak in tongues once. I was twenty-five and in the heart-wrenching process of ending a close relationship. Jim and I had been involved for almost a year, and he had decided that he wanted to go to graduate school in England. We had already been drifting apart for several months. I was in a very confused place trying to figure out my career and working temp jobs ~ doing menial administrative work far below my qualifications.

Since my sense of worthiness and identity was so bound up in the work I did, I was feeling like a failure and in no way willing to follow Jim to wherever his next destination was. It felt like his ego was swallowing my fragile identity, and I knew I needed to find my own path independently. Yet he had shown me a love and touched my soul as no one had before. We were both in so much pain over knowing that we needed to end our bond that we sought out various churches together for some answers. One of them was a growing evangelical church.

At one point in the service that Sunday morning, a whole group of people on one side of the church began to wail and shout out in a very odd language. The energy in the service had been building up with singing and the minister's entreating us to find God. As the people started speaking out, the minister supported them and asked us to pray with them as they were "talking with God."

It was too weird for me. I can't say that going to that service helped Jim and me. I walked away with a lasting impression and more unanswered questions that fed my inner dissonance. And Jim and I were left still searching for a semblance of love and inner peace to transcend the anguish of our deeply wounded hearts.

Yet Mary spoke in tongues and had a grasp of some spiritual truth in her life. I could see it in her eyes. The joy she had in reading her message to me. She was truly excited to be sharing her beliefs with me. I think part of it was her hope that I would be the one who conveyed her message out to the world.

It was heartening to hear Mary talk about her spiritual vacuum in her late teens. Isn't it the majority of us who experience this? And she found God so young. I was lost in confusion for far more years than she was.

I was also rather envious of how easy it seemed for her once she found God. She was so happy to slip into the mold that the Apostolic Church provided her. It seemed that her minister gave her all the answers. Even some of the statements she made in the interview sounded like direct quotes from her minister. "Heart surgery." It must be so nice to not question teachers as I habitually do.

Mary also had community, a powerful spiritual community. I so yearned for that. At the time of the interview, my spiritual vacuum was very real inside me. I also love to sing, and Mary invited me to go to one of her church services with her. I was actually considering joining their choir so that I could feel that glorious energy of deep spiritual singing.

Once I arrived at her church, however, I doubted this was going to be my spiritual community. I was the only white person in the whole service and was very under-dressed. All the women were decked out in their fanciest of fancy. I was in simple slacks. Everyone was staring at me, politely ~ but still staring. I knew my closet was woefully short on these types of dresses. Nor did I even like to dress like that. I realized that I did not have the right wardrobe for this congregation, nor was I comfortable being in the minority.

When the service started, there were prayers and singing, which was rather glorious. Partway through, people were asked to come forth. The next thing I knew, people were kneeling at the railing in the front and sobbing to God. Other people were holding them and praying loudly. Someone was trying to heal from his years of drugs. Another person had led a life of sin ~ I'm not sure which sins. The whole scene was a bit too emotional for my reserved nature.

I don't even remember what happened after that. All I know is that that clinched it for me. When the service was over, I tried to be as gracious as I could in thanking Mary for hosting me. I did not have the heart to tell her that I did not think I would be back. But I think she knew.

One thing that Mary said ~ that I carry with me ~ is the idea that God's love created the natural world. She was not the first to have expressed that, but she reminded me. Sometimes when I feel so unloved and desolate, I look out at the trees around my house and wonder if they could emanate that love and I could feel it. Perhaps if I try hard enough or flick the right switch in my emotions, my heart could take in the love that is behind those towering branches and solid trunk. If only it were that easy.

Sometimes, when I'm alone in the woods, I'll walk up to a tree and still myself and touch it. I really think I can feel something. A subtle warmth that comes over my heart. A little more peace. A deeper stillness, perhaps. Maybe a tiny glimpse of that divine love that helps me realize that the trees are my community as much as any person. And, in truth, I am never alone.

✧

baltimore, maryland
may 1996

dear God...

   this is the morning of my younger sister's wedding. i woke up feeling anxious, afraid of the depth of my feelings today. my shoulders feel tight and i caught myself breathing very shallowly.
   the man i thought i liked has not called me for two weeks and i, again, feel terribly rejected. i don't want to go to the wedding. i don't want to see anyone, especially all my family and their friends. all i want to do is hide.
   after the rehearsal dinner last night, i came home feeling so woeful, so full of shame because i am single. when i'm out doing errands, i see women younger than i am with their young children. how is it that they can handle a relationship, marriage and children? (although maybe they can't?) why does love come so easily to them and not to me?
   but I could never have a child right now. i don't have the emotional strength to take care of one. my other younger sister, sharon, had her second child this year. when she gave birth, it was very difficult for me. i couldn't even stay to visit her for very long at the hospital for fear i'd burst into tears being near her holding the baby. the suppressed desire I have to carry a child and give birth started to surface and overwhelm me. she could see what i was going through and was very gentle with me in spite of her exhaustion from her recent delivery.
   i try to deny this pain of not being involved with anyone, but in times like now, i feel the wave of it all coming back over me to swallow me up. like jonah and the whale, but in my case, my whale is the sorrow that has swallowed me. at least jonah could hide successfully that way.
   this winter i found some housemates to share the tenant house here on the farm. it was a couple who were very committed to their

97

buddhist path. they were really wonderful, spiritual people who cared deeply for each other. they've been good teachers of how loving a couple can be. their spiritual work is important to them also. they meditated often in front of a lovely altar set up in one corner of their bedroom. but much as i admire their path, it does not feel right for me. they have just moved out since my farm-sitting stint is over next week. i miss them already.

so, God, i'm leaving baltimore and heading to new england for the summer. i'm going to garden at the Omega Institute, a holistic education center that offers workshops on self-discovery for adults and families. it should be an interesting place; they have all sorts of workshops from meditation to theatre and dance to shamanic rituals. more than anything, i'm looking forward to being in their gardens all day. beyond the summer at Omega, i'm not sure. all i know is that my life has not come together in baltimore. i lived with judith and then farm-sat on this gorgeous farm, but i haven't made many friends and i don't feel any pull to stay here.

please guide me, God. i need Your help.

i give You my humble love,
Your daughter,

mare

CHAPTER 10

GRACE

TOM PRINSTER
AGE: 51

I HAVE NO OBJECTION TO CHURCHES
SO LONG AS THEY DO NOT INTERFERE
WITH GOD'S WORK.

~ BROOKS ATKINSON

In May of 1996, I left Baltimore to garden at the Omega Institute for the summer. Working at Omega was a great adventure, with a multitude of fun activities and interesting people to meet. The staff was an eclectic mix of free spirits and spiritual seekers. Friendships came easily there. Many of us, including myself, lived in our tents in the woods. The gardens were extensive, and my fellow gardeners covered a broad range of ages and life experiences. Between sleeping in my tent at night and gardening all day, I was quite happy being around more like-minded people and spending the bulk of my time in nature.

One of the advantages of working at Omega is that the staff eats in the same dining hall as the guests and presenters. Meal conversations had the potential to be quite stimulating, depending on which new workshops were being held that week.

Partway through the summer, I joined several workshop attendees for lunch in the dining room. They were all in the same healing program. One of the men captured my attention because of his physical scars, but I tried to be discreet about looking at him after I introduced myself to everyone. His name was Tom Prinster.

Tom's beard only partially covered the burn scars on his cheeks and chin. It was with great effort that he got up from the table. As he walked, he hunched over with a limp and used a cane to support himself. It was clear that Tom had been in some type of accident. His good looks were still there, though ~ a handsome, tall, dark-haired man with a strong sensitive presence ~ in spite of his scars and physical limitations.

Tom and I struck up a personal conversation while eating together. Since he was at the center for a week-long workshop, I saw him several more times at meals and made an effort to join him. He seemed to be a very kind person. One night we continued our conversation beyond dinner, and I found the courage to ask him how he had gotten all of his scars.

Tom had been a commercial pilot in New England in the early '80s. One early winter's day, he was assigned to pilot a small commuter shuttle between Groton, Connecticut, and Boston. Shortly after takeoff, he needed to turn on the de-icing fluids. Moments afterwards he smelled smoke, and flames burst through the cockpit floor, engulfing him and the copilot.

He radioed the nearest airport but knew he did not have time to fly the plane that distance. He spotted a frozen lake below the plane and thrust his hands through the flames to pilot the plane onto it. The plane lost a wing in the landing, and he jumped through the window as soon as it came to a halt on the ice. Moments after he escaped, the pain hit him and he realized that he was very seriously injured. One of the passengers died of smoke inhalation, while the rest of the crew and passengers escaped with some injuries. He had to go through two years of reconstructive surgery before he could lead a relatively normal life.

I got the sense that Tom had lived several lifetimes since that accident. He was at the holistic center attending a workshop on a body-mind healing approach to complement his recent master's degree in psychology. I'm not sure what other work he had done since the accident. He was returning to his home in the Southwest to start a practice at the end of that summer. I had a feeling that he was going to be a successful therapist with his deep sensitivity and empathic presence.

✧

If I gave you God's phone number, what would you do with it?

First of all, I would dial the number. Then I would wait to see what would happen. And if God answered, I'd have a dialogue.

We'd probably start by doing the polite things like, "How are you doing?" He/She/It would say, "I'm doing fine. How are you doing?" That sort of stuff. And then, well, I would be a little bit embarrassed. I'd have to ask God about the gender thing in a subtle way to clear that up. Actually, I think He/She/It would feel insulted if I were to ask about His/Her gender. It seems to me that He/She/It would not want to converse on these fairly simple and stupid terms.

But if God were comfortable conversing on this level?

I guess then I'd ask, "Did you create the bad things as well as the good things?" I have always wondered about bad and good. I was taught as a little kid that God would give you things if you prayed. I see that mentality all around me even now. That's the common interpretation of prayer. You pray and God gives you things. It's the kind of thing that's ingrained in us from our Christian culture ~ like it is ingrained in us that God is all-powerful and created everything in the universe.

So anytime anything good happens, you say, "Thank God." But then I wonder why a person down the street doesn't say, "Thank you, God," when they get a disease, or a broken arm, or bankruptcy.

Did He create all of our situations, including evil ones? If He did, I'd want to ask, "Why did you bother creating this world if there is so much evil in it?"

What do you think God might say back to you if you asked Him that question?

I think that He would be insulted with that question, too, if this were truly a God that I could converse with over a phone. This God that I had on the phone would be brought right down to a nuts-and-bolts level having to explain for something that He had done ~ such as creating evil. He'd have to be responsible at a human level. And if this God I got on the phone got into this level of explaining, I think this would make Him not God.

I really think this is why the Catholics needed Christ. Christ was an intermediary who could answer those questions, and God couldn't. God is supposedly above the whole mess.

I mean I guess I could ask God these questions, but I don't think I'd get a hell of an answer, though! [Laughs] It would probably be more like a big, thundering silence on the other end!

I really think that if there is one God out there, somewhere, that God would be removed from any sort of dialogue with me and my tiny little ego asking silly questions like: "What is your gender?" and "Did you create good and evil?" And that's the only way I could see God being. Because if God could dialogue with me over the phone, He would have to buy into the same rules of dialogue, of rationality, of "yes" and "no" and "maybe" human discourse. But I don't think God would want to do that, if God were God, like people like to believe He's God.

But right now you've got this God on the phone...

I guess I have real trouble with this concept that I could get this God on the phone. I think that's a cultural thing, this perception of God that could be called on the phone. For one thing, I think people find it necessary to think that there is a God. I don't think it's a personified thing for everyone, but I think most people need to conjure up the possibility of a God.

Whether there is a God or not is not really the issue. But if people go through life and what gets thrown to them eternally is that there is a God out there somewhere, this set of beliefs becomes a real, simple knee-jerk reaction to a lack of meaning in life. You ascribe the whole business to an author. You externalize your responsibilities. And if there weren't a God, then you would have to face tremendous anxiety and responsibility, and you would have to get off your ass and do a lot of things to go out and create good.

I mean, people are told to believe, "This is what God intended. Yes, God did intend AIDS, and cancer, bankruptcies, Thalidomide babies, and the war in Bosnia-Herzegovina. It's God's intent. We don't have to do anything."

I think that's really a poisonous attitude. It's been my experience that believing in the Christian God outside myself, all-powerful and all-good and all-bad plants a lot of lies. It doesn't work anymore for me.

I truly believe that this Christian God outside us is

fairly fundamentalist stuff. The more people move away from that paradigm of saying that there's a God out there, the better. The further away people come from miracle making, saving the day or investing power in an entity other than themselves, and the more they invest power inside themselves, then the more good they will do for the world.

But this belief in an external God is still tremendously embedded in our culture, and the far right greatly exploits that politically and socially. I think it's a great palliative for the man on the street not to have to think he's responsible for making moral choices. "Just look it up in the Bible, it's right there. You don't have to think."

So it sounds like you are not too comfortable with the idea of a phone number to God.

This just does not work for me. The God that I assume for myself exists as a state of mind and is an internal entity for me. Once in a while I can contact that God, and it feels like grace. I feel that grace inside myself when I'm aligned in my head and my heart and my body as I want. When the circumstances and everything is aligned and my ego is not in whatever's happening, I can sense the presence of something other than myself. I can sense the presence of a God, what people might call a God. It's a power other than me that exists inside me.

It's very rare that I get a glimpse of this inner God or grace. When I've cleared enough of the external crap away, then I am aware enough internally to sense it. I do think I've seen other people experience this grace when I've seen a healing in a workshop. But those workshops usually involved someone who has been trained to guide their client toward the God within, the grace. I think a good therapist or good shaman can do that.

So if someone gave me a phone number and told me

that it was God's number, I would go along with it and dial the phone number. I'd want to see what happens, see who answered it. [Laughs dryly] Maybe I'd get a lollipop or something. You never know.

And if I really got God on the phone, the questions that I was thinking that I might ask God before don't really pertain. They're not really questions that I would ask. They depend on the idea of a God outside of yourself, a power outside of yourself. And that's what I can't buy into.

I think these older beliefs were a necessity a couple of thousand years ago. I think the early Western culture shifted in such a way that there had to be one transcendental God. Our culture separated the one God outside the human realm, and this God moved beyond language and beyond touch and beyond the five senses. I assume that that's what would be meant by a God that's going to answer a phone call.

Would it be possible to make a phone call to the God that you know now?

No, that just does not work. It would be like mixing two dimensions. When you reach outside and you touch the dial on the phone, you're reaching into a three-dimensional place. My God is an inner God and does not obey those rules. This inner God is a psychic entity.

I do have conversations with this inner entity at times, but it is not like a phone call. I converse through my dreams once in a while. These are not real conversations, but there are messages that come through images very clearly. Sometimes the messages come with the themes of the dreams that I have. And when my dreams leave me and I can't remember them, I feel it as a tremendous loss. And when I listen in that way, I get guided gently. It fills me up, makes my life richer. It adds meaning to my life. That's important.

It's not easy for me to tap right into that inner space ~ that grace. It depends on how quiet I can get ~ and how important it is. There are always some things that remain unanswered that I just have to bluff my way through.

Like right now, I'm going to have to leave my course here at Omega early. My father's at a very critical point with his cancer, and I don't know how to deal with it. I've watched my dreams the last two weeks knowing that the family is going to be gathering. That unfinished business I have with my sister is there big time and the fears and the undone stuff with my father is there, but I don't have any answers.

And I just have to wait and not do anything stupid. I don't pray. I just wait. I've learned to be with my fears and the experience of them and not ignore them, to just see and pay attention in a receptive way. I guess some people might call this receptivity feminine energy. That's hard to do, but I try to guide myself like that.

I lived in a state of reaction for so many years. Somebody does something. You do it back. It's a stupid way to do things. It just hands a pile of shit back to the guy who gave it to you. I'm trying to change that because it just doesn't work anymore. You know I have to wait. I can't just call God up for an answer and have an answer be there. It doesn't work that way.

Hmmm...Do you suppose that some of your beliefs have come from your accident?

Yes, probably. It's beyond words. But when that cockpit caught on fire, it was as if I was not the one doing the flying. There was something else there.

What I mean is that I watched myself do what I did. I did stuff that would terrify me now if I thought that I had to do it again, breathing the smoke, putting my hands into the flames, keeping them there. I didn't feel any pain in the moment. There was no sense of panic or hurry, and I did everything right, and I can't believe that I did that.

It was as if there were another person there besides me ~ the guy in the seat getting all burned up. Another consciousness and another awareness. I don't know what that was. I don't want to name it. It just happened that way. There was an intelligence apart from me, watching me do what I was doing. I have that memory.

When I came out of that and became more grounded, literally, I wasn't capable of proceeding like that anymore. I went back to how I was before. I would do things, not watch myself, but simply be in the doing of it. And I'd have fears and doubts and not know what to say and be the normal human that I was before the accident.

I guess when I talk about the God within, that could have been some piece of it, some manifestation of it, but I don't know, once you name it, then you've damaged it, so I'm just saying what happened. I'm hesitant to name that sort of thing.

I've heard of people with the same sort of observing intelligence who do evil things. They have the same sort of detachment but use guns and violence and that sort of thing with the same dispassionate witness state.

It simply happened for me. If it was God, then I do believe that God has an evil face, too. And God empowers evil doings with this witness ability also. Or you've got to give Him or Her credit for that. I don't have any answers. I just hold that and proceed with my life the best I can.

That's really fascinating...

Did that clear it all up about God? I guess I'm saying, I don't think I could converse with an entity. I'm fairly straight about where God is for me...But that It's not out there ~ outside of me ~ for me. I really have never heard of an external God who would really pick up a phone. I've seen no evidence of that.

Not too many people have! (Laughing) Tom, can you tell me a little bit about how you were raised?

If you really want to understand where I'm coming from...I was raised Catholic. I went to Catholic grade school and then three years of a Catholic college. [Laughs] Been in recovery ever since!

✧

As I interviewed Tom, I was struck by how strong he was. Here was a man who had been through some extremely challenging life experiences and had continued to open his heart and keep on living, keep on growing.

Tom's plane accident was extreme. I certainly don't know what happened when he felt a consciousness outside of himself guiding the plane to land on the ice. Perhaps it was his spirit guide taking over as his body went into shock. I have heard of these types of things happening. Catholics might call it the work of the guardian angel. Whatever it was, it truly seemed to be something in the spirit world assisting him.

It was interesting to hear him talk about his experiencing grace at times. Perhaps this is the same experience that I call bliss when I feel deeply connected to God, although Tom did not want to put a name on it.

I suppose this is what many people try to achieve through meditation or deep prayer ~ that sense of oneness ~ complete alignment with an inner sense of the divine in their stillness.

There is a song that deeply speaks to this inner God that I hear in my head sometimes. The song is called Be Still and Know, and it is a hauntingly beautiful piece. It was inspired by Psalm 46:10. The lyrics include:

Be still and know,
Be still and know that I am God.
Be still and know that I am here.
Be still and know that I love you.

It repeats the "Be still and know" refrain over and over, and whenever I listen to it, it truly shifts my heart to a more open place. The song is one of the last vestiges of Kripalu Yoga Center that I still turn to occasionally to remind of me of that inner God. The words encourage me to remember that I know that God is within me as bliss and that I can experience It.

I don't have a meditative or prayer practice, although I do sit in front of my small altar in my bedroom to still myself every night. In those moments of calm, it seems that I can lift myself out of whatever difficult emotions I may be caught up in, to allow myself to perceive my life as one close to God and Earth Mother and their love. I temporarily transcend my mind clutter of mundane thoughts and remember ~ remember that the spiritual side of me is wiser than the mental and physical.

I guess one could say that this is my time every day that I devote to calling God. Except that I don't just call God but I also call Earth Mother. I call both of them and let them know that it is I calling them and thank them, and then I try to be still inside to hear whether any wisdom comes through to teach me in the moment. Sometimes I receive some wisdom and sometimes I don't. One time when I was feeling hurt by a friend and was having a hard time understanding why she would not talk with me, I heard something close to "Keep your heart open and have patience." Another time I actually heard that the reason I bought my house was so that I would be able to focus on writing this book there. I never know what I'm going to hear.

Many times I can't calm my thoughts, so I don't hear

anything. So I just accept that and crawl into bed hoping that sleep will bring me some stillness or even some answers. But usually I receive some insight that puts me more at peace, and I can then get ready for bed feeling more connected with my higher self or my divine side.

CHAPTER 11

GIVE EVERYONE THE SPIRIT

STEZI MAZIBUKO
AGE: 42

THE WIND BLOWS WHERE IT WISHES.
YOU HEAR THE SOUND IT MAKES, BUT YOU
DO NOT KNOW WHERE IT COMES FROM OR
WHERE IT IS GOING. IT IS LIKE THAT WITH
EVERYONE WHO IS BORN OF THE SPIRIT.

~ JOHN 3:8

S tezi Mazibuko is a member of Ladysmith Black Mambazo. Ladysmith Black Mambazo is an all-male choral group from South Africa that first became known in the USA when Paul Simon arranged for them to accompany him on his Graceland album. Stezi was raised in South Africa and now performs around the world with the internationally acclaimed singing group.

Ladysmith Black Mambazo was at Omega for several days, a layover between concerts. Their visit was spur of the moment for the Institute, so the staff had to scramble to find rooms and arrange a concert for them. They also gave a workshop solely for staff where we learned several of their songs and dance routines. It was great fun.

I thought that it might be interesting to interview a singer in the group. So I asked one of the Omega administrative staff if he felt comfortable with my approaching a band member to ask. He had no problem and directed me to speak with Joseph Shabalala, the leader of the group. I sought out Joseph later that same day, and he was very enthusiastic about the idea and asked if I could interview everyone in the group. I was a bit taken aback by his request and told him it was not possible since they were leaving in two days and I had to work during the day. Joseph understood and recommended that I talk to one particular singer, Stezi. He said that he would ask Stezi for me and let me know. Later that day at dinner, Joseph introduced me to Stezi, a very dark-skinned, fit-looking man of medium height. I was immediately touched by Stezi's shy but warm smile. We arranged a time to talk the next day.

English is not the first language for the singers in Ladysmith Black Mambazo, so when Stezi and I met for the interview the next day, I had to listen very closely to his thick Swazi accent to understand his English.

✧

If I gave you God's phone number, what would you do with it?

Well, I would call Him.

You'd call him...What would you want to say to Him?

First of all, I would ask Him for blessings because I would like to be blessed in everything I do. Like when I'm working, I want that work to be blessed.

Then I would ask for life, to give me long life, to stay on Earth for a long time.

Then I would ask Him to do away with things that are bad, like flood...tornadoes...thunderstorms...all those things that bother us.

[Pause]

I would also ask Him to give people love so that they can learn to love each other.

Would you want to ask Him any questions?

What else should I ask... [long silence] Let me think what else. [More silence] I cannot think of anything else...

I guess I could ask Him some questions about my parents. They died when I was in my early twenties. I could ask God why did He let them die when I was so young. I thought I would grow up and work to support them. I thought I would make them proud of me because we were so poor when I was young. But they died so early.

What do you think He might say back to you if you asked Him about why they died when they did?

Maybe He would say it was their time to die. I think we are not all supposed to die at the same age. Everyone reaches a certain age and then dies. Some die young...Some die when they're too old. I think He would say it was the time for them to die.

It was their time...Is there anything else?

[Long silence] Let me think...Yeah, I would ask Him why did He create people so that they can do what they like? He's supposed to create them in such a way that He can control them, like people control their TV with a remote. He's supposed to not let people do what they like because sometimes people do bad things. God does not like bad things.

What do you think God might say back to that question?

Oh, maybe He would say that He wanted people to be free because He created people in His image and then He wanted them to enjoy the freedom while they were on Earth. Maybe He would say He didn't know that there would come a time when the people would be out of control. People are killing each other unnecessarily, hating each other even though we are all in His image. That's a problem!

Maybe He would say that He gave us minds to decide between the bad and the good. He thought we'd like to do good things and take some examples from Him. We are not like animals. We are people, so we know what is bad. We know what is good. He's given us the ability to choose, and yet some people still choose to do bad things.

Hmmm, yes, they do...Any other questions?

Maybe I could ask him to do away with incurable diseases like AIDS and cancer. AIDS is very, very big in South Africa.

Do you think God would have an answer for you if you asked him about diseases?

Yeah, with AIDS, maybe He would answer that He didn't create us to have many partners. He created a man to have his own wife, not to look around and to sleep around. I can't say that it's a punishment but perhaps something we get because we don't obey His rules.

Maybe many of these diseases are a curse since we did not obey His rule from the beginning when He created Man and Woman. Maybe this is why He let us have so many diseases after we left the Garden of Eden.

That's interesting...Maybe He would. Hard to imagine what life would be like if we all had stayed in the Garden of

Eden. Tell me, Stezi, do you go to church when you are back in South Africa?

Yes, I go to the Church of God. It's a Christian evangelical church. Everyone in Ladysmith Black Mambazo goes to this church. We go every Sunday.

This is not the same church that I went to when I was a boy. My mother and my uncle would take me to an Anglican Church. But I lost interest as I got older. I started to play soccer on Sunday mornings instead.

But after Joseph [Shambalala, the leader of Ladysmith Black Mambazo] repented and joined the church in 1976, he started preaching to us in the group then as if he was our own minister. He asked forgiveness for all his sins and was baptized in the church ~ that is repenting. Joseph used to take us to the church and ask us to sit there. I repented in 1977.

Did you have a spiritual experience when you repented and joined the church?

Yes, I had a spiritual experience...I felt that there's something, ah, how should I put this? [Pause] ...I felt there's something connecting me and God...When I pray now, I feel there is spirit leading me to pray more and more.

It is not like when I was young when I wondered what I would say in my prayers. There was no feeling that I was talking to God at that time. But after I started to listen to Joseph, I started to feel the spirit. And I started to go back to church. I feel the spirit often now when I am in church.

That's wonderful. Are there any other times in your life that you feel that spirit, perhaps during the week when you are not at church?

Yeah, yeah...sometimes I just feel it. When I'm maybe

sitting alone just with the spirit. I feel it when I'm singing sometimes, but I don't know what kind of spirit it is. I felt that spirit when I would sing before I joined the church. But now something inspires me when I sing to sing more. I cannot tell if it is the same spirit that inspires me to go to church or be alone or be with God.

Before I repented, I would feel the spirit when I was on stage and the song was good. Sometimes I would feel it if we were practicing and the song was coming along all right, but not every day. If we were just learning a song and we were not sure, I would not feel it. I do feel it more now when we are practicing and the song is good.

Yeah, maybe another thing I can ask from God is to give each and everyone the spirit.

How would you ask for that? Would you just say: "God, give them the spirit"?

I would ask Him to give the people the spirit so that they can feel and know that there is God in them. Give them energy to do good things.

Maybe He'd say that He already gave some the spirit. He might say you have to go to those people of the spirit and join them so that you can have the spirit as well. These are people who go to church and pray and see things before they happen. They can profess what is going to happen. Some pray for the sick and they become well. Those are people who have the spirit. There are people at my church who do that.

I think God would say to go find those people and spend time with them. Like in olden days when nations would have prophets to tell them what God said. The people would have to listen to that person.

It sounds like you go to a very interesting church.

Yeah. Some people ~ not everyone ~ in the church can do that. I think it's their gift. I can't say why they have the gift. It's just their gift.

What else can I ask God? I don't know...I think blessing us is the most important thing because whatever you do, if you have blessing, you will succeed.

I think that would be it. I would say: "Thank you." Since talking to God directly is an honor. And then I would say: "Goodbye. Thanks for the conversation. Talk to you next time when I remember something."

✧

This interview with Stezi felt almost mystical. It was one of those rare interviews where it felt like "spirit" entered our space as we talked. Even when I re-listen to the tape, I experience it. As Stezi continued to open up and talk more, especially about his singing, I was shifted into a deeper, more God-connected space. It was almost as though a bubble formed around us where God's spirit or love enveloped us. I was sad when the interview was over for I could feel the bubble dissipate as we both got up and walked out of the room.

One thing that Stezi mentioned was that God might instruct people to find those with the spirit ~ those "who go to church." In reflecting on that, I've realized that I've met incredible people of spirit who are both churchgoers and non-churchgoers. Some of the most spiritual people I have met do not set foot in a church, but they may garden or do carpentry professionally. These people tend to work with their hands, and their work is a spiritual practice.

I think most of us can feel when we are around people like this. They emanate a warmth and compassion that pulls us to them. They certainly pull me to them. I just want to hug them and take them home with me so that I can soak up more of their inner love and wisdom ~ a wisdom and a spiritual connection they seem to have developed primarily outside of any religious structure.

I also loved that Stezi would ask God to give people His spirit. I wondered if this could be the same as giving them the knowledge that God loves them. This has been one of the most profound revelations for me ~ to deeply integrate the knowledge that God loves me. As a Presbyterian minister friend of mine terms it: "You are beloved."

In all my bouts with depression, my poor self-esteem was at the core of much of my suffering. When I did self-help workshops, the inner work that always surfaced was to quell the inner voice that continuously repeated: "I am not good enough." As I got stronger and more secure in my spiritual beliefs, I began to realize that God loved me. Truly accepting that meant that I was good enough, for God loves me as I am ~ not as I should be. This was such a liberating awareness since it meant that I no longer needed to try to please others or work harder for that next level of recognition ~ so that others would think I was good enough.

What an incredible world this would be if all those drug addicts, alcoholics, workaholics ~ all those people out there who grapple with a feeling of emptiness inside ~ could be given the spirit. If they could be given that feeling of love within themselves to always tap into when they felt discouraged, surely our global community on Earth would be closer to God.

WHAT IF GOD'S HAVING A CYNICAL DAY?

Eric Rosen*

Age: 21

WE ARE GOD'S PARTNERS IN THE ACT OF
CREATION. TO SHAPE THE NATURAL
ENVIRONMENT WISELY, WE SHOULD APPROACH IT
WITH REVERENCE. LET US AWAKEN OURSELVES
BEFORE IT IS TOO LATE!

~ JAN GRZESICA AND ALEXEY YABLOKOV

Eric Rosen and I were on the staff together at the
Omega Institute during the summer of 1996. After days
of working side by side in the garden, we developed a
strong kinship. Perhaps it was our love of poetry or
fascination with the Monty Python and The Holy Grail movie.
Regardless, we became good friends that summer.

When I met Eric, my initial impression was that we would
never get along. An athletic-looking young man of medium
build, he had a miniature barbell piercing the center of his
tongue, and his dark hair was growing out in dreadlocks. He
looked like a guy with little sense of responsibility. I had no
idea that he was a very serious academic at the time.

---

*not his real name

It turned out that Eric was about to start his senior year at Duke University. His academic advisor there had accelerated him into graduate-level work on a German philosopher. His goal was to apply to graduate schools for a Ph.D. in literature and philosophy after college.

Once I got beyond the tongue barbell (he shared that his previous girlfriend pierced people's bodies for a living and that he had other body parts pierced also), I found Eric to be quite fun. After many long hours of conversation together, we found that we had a very similar sense of humor. We cracked jokes and put on ridiculous British accents to imitate characters from Monty Python and The Holy Grail. It got to the point where some of the other staff at Omega started avoiding us at meals because they couldn't appreciate our odd sense of humor.

Eric was a very gifted poet and had a wacky sense of humor. In a strange way, I enjoyed his radical ways. Not that I always agreed with him. He had already sized up the world and was confident in his views. In sum, "The world is fucked."

Some of his radical bohemian ways went beyond my place of comfort. I could not understand his self-mutilation, bisexuality and need for drugs ~ he loved to smoke pot and take LSD. Eric seemed to have the need to be out on the extreme edge. An avid rock climber, he nearly died from a rock fall just three days before we did the interview. He was covered with scratches and large, dark bruises for several weeks following.

Eric was actually a very productive young man, as I learned. While in college, he managed the newspaper subscriptions for all the students on campus as a business on the side. In his off-off-time, he edited the college poetry journal and played Ultimate Frisbee, a form of Frisbee soccer. He spent his late hours smoking pot, drafting poetry or sleeping with his present lover, a woman, in the house he shared with his six housemates.

In the course of our many conversations, Eric shared a bit of his background. His parents were divorced and both remarried. His father was a very successful lawyer, and his mother had remarried a wealthy businessman. His mother and stepfather and grandparents were heavily involved in their Jewish religion.

Eric knew that I was working on the book from some of our conversations. Six weeks into the summer I finally asked him if he was willing to be interviewed. He was very willing.

✧

If I gave you God's phone number, what would you do with it?

I'm not sure what I would do with God's phone number. I get this image of a God sitting behind a desk and answering calls with a phone headset on. This is definitely not how I imagine God.

The idea of an external God that may be able to answer a phone has strong Christian implications to me. I'm not sure about an incarnate God that we can communicate with. There are people out there who will swear that Jesus is the Son of the Father and the Savior to their life. But my Jewish background tells me otherwise.

There is definitely something mysterious that I can't explain that brought us where we are. I believe in the Spirit. I think that we do go around.

What do you mean "We go around"?

Perhaps in reincarnation.

If I were given the power to call God, it would have to be a very significant moment. I would assume that when the time came to use it, another dawn of knowledge might come to me, and I might then be inspired to know how to use it.

But maybe you have your own motivation for disseminating this number. You could be collecting a society. You could be telling me you're giving me God's number and it could be the Devil's instead! [Laughs]

But that's one of the criteria ~ the number is to God.

But what you define as God and what I define as God may be entirely different things. Who's to say what your God is? It could be the Lady of the Lake in King Arthur's legends. [Laughs]

Even if you promised me that the phone number is to my God, this doesn't work for me. I'm not so sure that there is a God. Maybe there is. Even still, I wouldn't call God up and ask Him or Her about too many things. There are some things I don't think I want answers to. I may not be ready for the information God might give me and get hurt by it instead.

I've read about yogis who have given divine information about how to peer directly into the sun to disciples who begged and begged for it. Then the disciples burned their eyes out because they weren't truly ready for the knowledge.

I really think we need to learn explicitly through experience. Calling God would be like a "get out of jail free" card. It would be an easy out. Suppose you get yourself in a really bad mess and you need an answer. You call God's number and get a direct answer. You don't have to work for it or learn anything from your mistake. I'm not so sure that this would be helping us.

I am assuming that God would give us some kind of response. I'm assuming that there would not be silence and then a dead line on the phone. [Laughs] At least we're going to get the opportunity for some kind of Divine response.

The concept here is that you can actually dialogue with God.

Okay.

Suppose I wanted to ask God for the secret to riches on Earth. Of course I'm going for big questions because I'm talking to The Big Person. And God said, "No, you don't deserve it." Or He just responded negatively.

I could be feeling malicious and ask for a Holy War! God may say: "No! You are a bad person for asking."

Or I could call God and ask Him what the answer to peace is. He may or He may not give me an answer, depending on whether He thinks I'm ready for it. I might start to think I could control the world with the information. If He did give me an answer, maybe the answer isn't something that I'm capable of performing anyway. Do I lose a little faith? I could feel very empowered or totally discouraged.

The real altruist would give up the number. But then it would be abused.

How would it be abused?

The real altruist would make the number widely accessible, and this could be a problem. God's switchboard would be full. [Laughs]

And even if God's switchboard could handle all the calls, I wouldn't want that number to be in free circulation. That's for damn sure. It's a powerful number. It would be entrusting a lot of fickle people with a power that might not be predictable. It would scare me to think who else has it. I wouldn't want that switchboard to be clogged by questions from all the religious right-wing types. [More chuckling]

But it would really scare me. We have this whole deal with mediation from the truth going on in our society.

Clothes hide our sexual responses. Words are never good enough to express our truth. And when honesty is told, it can be too shocking. Even the institutions in our lives protect us from the truth. Maybe it is better that way.

Calling God, the God, the Logos, means contacting the ultimate Source of Authority. I don't know if we would be ready for that level of truth. Whatever response we would get from the Creator of the Universe would carry a lot of potency. I'm not sure if it is good for us to have that kind of access to the ultimate Superego or the ultimate Conscious.

That is an interesting point.

I think a great deal about God and the permanence of our soul. I've had a recurring dream where I relive everything I have done over and over again. For example, I will sit and have the same lunch that I had today again, bite for bite. Whatever our eternity is, in my dreams it plays itself out repeatedly. I'm not certain whether we're here just for a brief nanosecond or we come back fifteen hundred times and end up being a Buddha.

Every moment in itself becomes a forever. This can be seen as bad and good. It's placed a burden on me for not absolutely taking advantage of every second because now I have the burden of eternity on every second. But at the same time it also takes away volition because if we're going to be here again, it's predestination, in a way. That's a conflict that I've been grappling with.

Then I've had other dreams where God is a ladybug. I've come upon this ladybug, and it's unlocking the secret to the universe through the polkadots on its back.

Were these dreams while you were asleep or taking drugs?

I dreamt these while I was sleeping.

But quite honestly we live in a world with pestilence and crime, and stars dwarfing and falling into black holes. God only knows where they go after black holes. We don't live in a perfect society. The only kind of insight that we have into a perfect society is through the myth that the universe was created in seven days and is about two thousand years old.

There are all kinds of beliefs. Some talk about Eden and that we are predestined to suffer. Others say we are misdirected and need to learn to love more. We all recognize that there could be more love.

But if this misdirection is not caused strictly by us and our foolishness, then has some Greater Being caused it? This means that this Greater Being has an evil side. Perhaps evil exists just by the duality of our nature. So then the question is whether Evil is separate from God or a duality in God?

Perhaps you would like to ask God about that?

This would be a good question to God. But I'm not sure I want the answer. It's just wide open. [Laughs]

It's very interesting. If God's a duality, what if He's having a cynical day? If God's not a duality, who's to say the Devil isn't tapping the line? [Laughs] If it's a clean line, who is the authority figure that keeps the line clean? Maybe God knows if the Devil's tapping Him and can change the channel. [Chuckle]

There are a lot of people on this Earth who believe in a God. I'm not so sure this is good. They fight over whose God is right as if God has certain qualities according to their specific doctrines. The Catholic God is a vengeful God, and the Jewish God is an angry God sometimes. And the Baha'i God is a beautiful, good God, and the Zoroastrian God is a God of something ~ I don't remember exactly what it is. But the Muslim God is a God that puts

Man on top always.

Ever since we've been able to articulate this Godhead, we've been fighting over it and killing each other. Native Americans were slaughtered since the settlers did not think the native people had a Godhead.

Suppose you were Catholic or Anglican and you were going on the Crusades. If they had phones back then, you could have called and asked God if the Crusades were a good idea. I'm relatively sure He would've said, "No, the Crusades are not a good idea." Then your entire faith is thrown into this questionable light, and you wonder if your God isn't going to save you, what God is? Maybe some of those people back then thought the Crusades were wrong. But a lot of them thought they were doing good. A lot of them got rich in the name of the Church, too.

There may have been people back then who questioned the Crusades...

Probably...But the Crusades are just one example of how popes have created some illogical decrees that all these people are compelled to follow. Even today, I'm not getting that abortions are bad from my dreams or talking with people. I'm not getting that condoms or premarital sex are wrong. Or that you should be giving alms to the poor. I get a lot of other messages in my dreams, but not those.

Think about it! If the Pope got hold of that phone number, God help us all! [Laughs] That's the final stage. If the Pope and the Cardinal School had their direct line to God...Watch out!

I'm relatively sure they don't have the number now. Maybe they do need it, though. It might encourage them to give up some of their infinite wealth to feed some people. Maybe they would right some of the pretty horrendous wrongs that they have subjected humanity to. I don't think there's any denying that this number is a powerful tool.

No, I don't think I'd use this number. I would buy a security box in a bank and put it in there. [Laughing loudly] I definitely wouldn't leave it in my wallet.

So you are saying that you would not use it at all.

I may pull the number out and use it if there were a natural disaster. Or to deal with some of our serious environmental problems. We're more or less denying all the environmental destruction going on. We're eating our ozone pretty fast. There's going to be a time in the future when people are going to say we were really stupid. At some point we cannot deny it. Maybe that's the moment when I call God. I could call Him now and ask for help, but I'm stubborn. I really want to see us pull out of this on our own.

Did you think about calling God for help when you fell rock climbing last weekend?

No. Although I definitely thought I was going to die while it was happening. Two people had died in that same place earlier in the year. All I could think was that this was a stupid way to go. I didn't ask for any help. I would not have called God. I would have been ready to go. I've lived twenty-one good years. I'm looking forward to death. It's the ultimate unknown.

[Pause]

There have been times I have asked God for help before, though. [Speaking very low] I've prayed to something out there when my little brother was dying from brain cancer. And I had a rough time growing up. After my parents divorced, my mother was a pretty miserable single parent. There were a couple of times when she sexually abused my brothers and me. I definitely asked why that was happening.

I also asked for help when I took the SATs and applied

to college. I did particularly well in school so it was kind of stupid for me to pray then. Another time was when our high school team was in the national hockey finals. Those were the most intense times of my life. I prayed for those games. I would never have called God to ask what was going to happen, though.

So praying is different from calling God?

Yeah. I think praying is hoping in an external way. You pray ~ you're looking for a ray of hope and trying to place the burden of that realization on somebody outside yourself. And calling God is a little more direct. [Laughs] A little less esoteric. More like, "Hey, God, what's gonna be the final score of the Bulls-Pistons game? I got this big bet going ~ I need to know!"

Think about it! What would happen if God's number got out to all the bookies. They'd be calling Him about every race. And what if God deceived them? What would that mean for them? [Laughs loudly]

I'm not sure, but I suspect that He would tell them: "Piss off. Don't call me about that stupid shit, and I'm changing my number tomorrow." [He says this with a mock British accent and laughs again.]

There would be all kinds of people calling if His number got out. It could be very, very interesting.

Okay. One last question: Do you go to temple very often now?

Well, I consider myself pretty spiritual. In terms of my being Jewish, though, I could count on two hands how many times I have been in the temple since my bar mitzvah. But I'm still very Jewish. You can take the boy out of the Jew, but you can't take the Jew out of the boy.

✧

This was a very intriguing interview. Eric brought up some very different angles on the concept of the phone number.

I was a bit surprised at his perception that this phone number could be abused. I had assumed that people would want to use such a number only for higher purposes. Yet he helped me realize that the darker side of humanity might see the number as a means for power.

Eric played with the concept of God's being cynical or negative, and this surprised me. It would never occur to me that God would have snappy answers for anyone who tried to communicate with Him. I believe God is far beyond being reactionary or mean. I do think He may be critical of the ignorance on our planet, with our current environmentally destructive patterns or extensive war habits. But I believe His consciousness sees what is happening globally now as part of the process that Earth is going through in its evolution.

Eric's comment about the Pope's getting hold of the number was quite something. I am convinced that many people feel that the Pope, of all people on Earth, does have the number. My father loves to tell me a joke about the gold phone that the Pope has which is a direct line to God for an exorbitant fee, while a simple Irish priest offers the same phone connection for free since it is a local call in Ireland.

Eric raised the possibility that the Vatican might actually relinquish much of its wealth to support poverty programs if it did have God's phone number already. Of course the assumption there is that God would instruct it to do that as the right thing. But from my limited understanding of Christ's teachings, it does seem that God and Christ would encourage the Vatican to live more simply and liquidate its assets to contribute to sound programs for the poor and sick. I have never understood how the Vatican can justify having such wealth.

It seemed to be difficult for Eric to show his vulnerability and share that he might seek help at times. Perhaps this was his young virile, male ego coming through. It was good to see that he could drop it at moments and be honest with me.

Another point that Eric made about the number giving us access to truth prompted me to think. He stated that we are constantly buffered from the truth. Perhaps it would be overwhelming for people to learn the real truth from God. And yet, isn't that what we truly seek, too?

I've reflected on Eric's point for a while since I'm known to be a direct person. I generally call things as I see them. There have been times that friends were not happy to hear my honesty. It has damaged a number of friendships and has forced me to grapple with whether I need to redefine what helping them means. What is the best way for me to be a friend to these people when I see what is happening? Probably a great question for God!

CHAPTER 13

WILL I BE SAVED?

NIKIA PHILLIPS*
AGE: 12

HAPPY ARE THOSE WHOSE GREATEST
DESIRE IS TO WHAT GOD REQUIRES:
GOD WILL SATISFY THEM FULLY.

~ MATTHEW 5:6

Shortly after I returned to Baltimore after the Omega Institute, I met a farm caretaker named Joseph who lived near my aunt's house. Joseph and his wife were from Trinidad, and they lived in a tenant house on a large horse estate.

I was hired to garden on the estate, so I ran into Joseph regularly. One morning I also met Joseph's twelve-year-old daughter from his first marriage, Nikia, who was visiting from Trinidad for several weeks. Nikia and Joseph's wife would walk discreetly around the gardens to collect the mail or find Joseph to give him lunch. They were both very timid and gave me gentle smiles when I waved to them.

I knew that I needed to interview more children, and the fact that Nikia was from a different country intrigued me. So one afternoon I asked Joseph whether he thought Nikia might be open to being interviewed. Joseph responded that he would ask her, which he did that night. The answer

---

*not her real name

was "yes." Nikia was so young and shy, it occurred to me afterwards that she might have felt she could not have said "no."

In any case, I walked over to the tenant house in the middle of the afternoon several days later. Nikia meekly met me at the door in rather starched formal church clothes. Her coarse dark hair was pulled back in a ponytail. When we sat down, Nikia buried herself deeply into the couch as I sat in the armchair next to it. During the interview, she nervously kept her small hands clasped tightly in her lap.

We chatted a little about her home and her family. She explained in her soft Trinidad accent that she lived with her grandparents there. They attended the Seventh Day Adventist Church regularly. She sang in the church choir and was active in different church projects.

$$\diamondsuit$$

If I gave you God's phone number, what would you do with it?

I would call Him.
I would ask Him how many sins I have committed and if I'll be saved.

What do you think He might say back to you?

I think He would tell me, "You've committed a number of sins, but I have forgiven you and you will be saved."
Then I would want to know about my family and friends and if they have committed sins and will be saved or not. Will they make it to God's Kingdom?

Nikia, what does it mean to be saved?

I think it means to go to Heaven and have eternal life with Jesus Christ and God.

And if you are not saved?

[In a meek voice] You will be burning in Hell.
[Pause]

Okay...So your hope is that God will be able to give you some kind of report on how everyone you know has been doing.

Yes. If He tells me that some of them are not going to be saved, I would ask him what I could do to try to make them be more righteous. I want them to see God and be saved. I think He'd tell me that I should talk to them about how good He is and about the wonderful miracles His son, Jesus, performed. If they don't listen, I'd just have to try again. I would try and try. If they don't want to listen, I'd have to give up.

Do you know people who you think might not be saved?

Yes. But I have not gone to them to try to help them see God. I didn't think they would listen to me. But if God told me over the phone that I could talk to them, I would.

Anything else?

I'd also ask Him how many days I have left to be on Earth. Death can take you anytime. It could be tomorrow or next week. God knows when it will happen. He would probably tell me that I have very many days left. I just have to be prepared for it.

I would also want to know if I am going to be a lawyer or doctor or be in a good profession like that. My main desire is to be a lawyer. I think God would say, "Just work hard on your studies of law, and you will get what you want."

Okay...Any more?

I could ask Him if I will go through any hard struggles between now and when I die... [pause] But God will probably say, "Yes, but try to keep up the faith and work your way through it." I need to hope and pray and believe that He will help me.

I wouldn't want to ask any more questions after that. I've already asked Him enough. I wouldn't want to pressure Him. I pray to Jesus and ask Him for many stuff already. When I pray, I hear an inner something, a voice, which is like God. Sometimes He tells me, "yes" and sometimes He tells me, "no." I follow it.

So I think I would want to end the phone call. But first I would ask God if I can call him back. I think He would say, "yes."

Would you do anything special with the number? Would you share it with anyone else?

I would keep the number and call back if I had a really big problem. I would also give the number to people who really wanted it.

The next time I called, I would like to ask to speak to His son, Jesus. I would want to ask Jesus if I can come see Him when I die. We could talk about his day. He may tell me he's encouraging some of the people who believe in him to go out and tell other people about him. He'd be having a good day. When people are not doing what they are supposed to do, it may be a bad day for him. That may happen.

✦

Nikia's way of thinking about God was so far removed from my beliefs that I was truly surprised by her words. On one hand, she had learned how to tap into an inner guidance that she called God. I thought this was exceptional for a twelve-year-old girl. On the other hand, some of Nikia's comments came from such a place of fear. Her foremost thoughts for God were whether she and her family and friends were going to be saved. It seemed that she was one of many young children who are raised to fear God and not feel God's love for them and experience joy instead.

There is a group of Jehovah's Witnesses that comes through my neighborhood on a regular basis knocking on doors and attempting to pull me into conversing with them. I just curtly say hi to them and tell them that I admire their persistence. I tried to tell one man who caught me working in the yard that I believe that there is God in everything, including the tree that I was weeding under. He just smiled at me strangely and said, "Have a nice day," and walked away.

They want to talk about the Bible with me, or so they tell me. My sense is that they truly believe that I am one of the un-saved but there is hope for me if I follow their path. But I actually feel very saved. I believe I'm living my life as Jesus would have wanted me to ~ with courage to reach my dreams and love toward others. I don't go to church, but I don't think that is the critical factor. It is my actions that count.

I am wary of religious groups that teach that they hold the only path to finding God, especially by instilling fear in their followers. I cannot believe that this is what Jesus wanted. I truly think that Jesus wanted us to live life with joy. He wanted us to be good, moral, ethical people who love God and know that God loves them. God does not want us to live in fear. He wants us to live in love and courage.

But I don't engage the suburban missionaries. I just wish them well. I'd much rather spend my time on a nice Saturday morning peacefully weeding my garden than trying to debate about God and religion with a stranger. But I sure wish that I could ask them to take my house off their list of stops just as I tell telemarketers to take my number off their list.

I think that being saved is actually saving ourselves from all the self-loathing that is so prevalent in our society and getting in touch with God's love for us. If more of us really realized how much God loves us, then we could sit in peace with ourselves and quell the emotional storms that rise within us when we've made mistakes or hurt someone. We would know how to forgive ourselves and not be so dependent on external love to weigh our worth.

I used to fall into deep despair if someone were angry with me. Large, red flashing neon failure lights went off in me. If a boyfriend broke up with me, I was devastated since my self-esteem was so small and the break-up surely meant that I was not a good person and hence not worthy of anyone's love. But as I gradually learned how much unconditional love the God/Creator has for me, I began to understand that I am a worthy person in spite of my weaknesses or the fact that I am without a lover again. I learned to save myself from my own self-persecution and hatred as I got in touch with all the love that the universe has for me. I think this is the real saving we need to get in touch with.

CHAPTER 14

SOMETHING MAKES
ALL THIS WORK

ISABELLE BUTLER*
AGE: 78

IN TIMES OF SUDDEN DANGER MOST PEOPLE
CALL OUT, "O MY GOD!" WHY WOULD THEY
KEEP DOING THIS IF IT DIDN'T HELP? ONLY A FOOL
KEEPS ON GOING BACK WHERE NOTHING HAPPENS.

~ RUMI

While I was still living with Judith, I met her close friend, Isabelle Butler. Isabelle visited Judith quite often. They had lived near each other in the same valley of rolling horse pastures and hay fields for over forty years.

An attractive woman of seventy-eight years, Isabelle always dressed elegantly in clothes that hugged her trim figure. Even if she were just stepping outside for a vigorous walk on the country lane, you would find her in smart casual clothes. She was a woman of class.

When Isabelle visited for a meal, I would often join her and Judith at the dining room table and listen in on the society gossip or the realities of widowhood in the proper country circles. Judith would lament how quiet her life had become and how few people invited her over for dinner.

*not her real name

But Isabelle's life was different. She kept her days full of social engagements. She loved to travel and went to Europe regularly. She was rather fearless about getting out of the house and taking in new adventures.

I loved to talk with Isabelle. She was friendly, and her forthrightness was refreshing and humorous. With a patrician air of authority, she always spoke her mind frankly and without hesitation. If you asked her how old she was, she had no qualms retorting: "How much money do you make?" She was not a woman who could be easily intimidated. Indeed, she was known to intimidate others.

I had wanted to interview Isabelle while I was still living with Judith because I knew she would be very up-front about her beliefs regardless of how controversial they might be. I also knew that she had some unique perspectives on God and death since we had chatted a little already. She laughed when I suggested doing an interview but was willing. I think she found the question rather funny. The challenge was finding a time to do it since she was so busy. Time passed, and we never got around to it while I was still living with Judith.

Then the following fall after I returned from Omega, I ran into Isabelle at a grocery store. We again discussed my interest in interviewing her, and she said she had some time over the weekend. So we met at my small apartment the following Sunday afternoon and finally conducted it.

✧

If I gave you God's phone number, what would you do with it?

Nothing. I'd think that you were slightly cuckoo if you told me that you had God's phone number. That's really what I would think. There is no such thing as a phone number to God. I really can't pretend that there is one.

And if there were, I wouldn't call. I wouldn't want to bother God because I'd think He had too many other people less fortunate than I to take care of.

And I know that His line would always be busy. I've been trying to get through to different companies to make repairs in one of the tenant houses on the farm. It's always a machine that answers, and they say to call back in twenty-four hours when the wires are less plugged. You can't get through to anyone anymore. So I wouldn't try God.

But suppose I told you that the line was always clear...

Even if the line were always clear and I was told God would answer, I wouldn't bother Him. I really haven't thought enough about Him. I wouldn't know what to ask.

To tell the truth, I haven't thought about God that much because I don't believe He exists. I think that every civilization craves and yearns for answers ~ for meaning. They yearn to think there must be something more than this because life is so miserable for most people in the world. They're so poor and so sick and so forlorn.

We're one-tenth of one percent of the world ~ we few privileged people. So most people have to think that there is something better than this world. It's so hard for them here. The women do nothing but bear children. It's just awful for most of them. They have to believe that there's something better coming.

But I think it's all right here. I don't think that there is any afterlife. I believe in Jesus because he was documented. He was a very charismatic man as a lot of ministers are. Most ministers who are successful are very charismatic. Their charisma turns people on, maybe even physically. I don't know. I mean ~ it's possible. There was a local minister whom my parents would go to listen to. Everyone loved him, and I think half the women were turned on by him. I know they were. Christ was a very charismatic man, and He had many followers because He was so charismatic. But that doesn't mean that God exists.

Then there are people who debate whether God's male, female or neuter. A lot of people think that He is a She now. That has destroyed my faith in Him even more.

But really...how could there be a Lord who could take care of everyone in the world? No spirit could. To think that the Lord could solve all of the world's problems is impossible.

Another reason ~ the main reason ~ I don't believe in God is that things are so unequal in life. So unfair. What about people who are born deformed? He would not allow that. Why is it that my children function perfectly but someone else was born without arms? It's not right.

There are more and more wars now. I don't think any Lord would want that to happen, either. I heard sometime last winter that there are fifty-four wars going on. And if you've ever been in the middle of a war, you can imagine how terrible that would be.

On the other hand, there is something that makes everything work so well in this world ~ the tides and the sun and the moon. The way things grow. The cycles of everything. Even after an earthquake or a forest fire. There was that big fire in Yellowstone a number of years ago, and all of that is growing back now. Things seem to right themselves, and that makes me believe that there is something that makes all this work. There are a lot of things that can't be explained, but I wouldn't necessarily call it God.

Would you give it another name?

No, no...I believe in nature. You have to believe in nature because we see it all the time. It's so fantastic. But, no, I don't believe in God.

When our children were young, I would take them to the Episcopalian Church nearby. I just felt that it was part of their education to go to church, and that was the closest one. But I wouldn't take communion. I just don't believe that Christ rose from the dead. I just don't believe all those things you say when you take communion, so I don't take it. I think it's just a form ~ an empty ritual ~ that most people follow because it is the thing to do. To a lot of people, it's very important and I don't know why.

I have a close friend, Jacqueline Clark*, who is very religious. Maybe too religious. She goes to Mass twice a day, and she does her rosary all the time. She devotes herself to it. She's charismatic in a way, but I think her beliefs are out of balance. First her husband died. Then her son died of cancer not too long afterwards. She took it all in stride without cracking up or giving into it. I wish I could do that. She has this complete faith that they've gone to Heaven ~ wherever that is ~ and the Lord has received them with open arms, and so forth and so on. She believes she'll see them all and recognize them when she gets up there. Who knows whether it's up there; it might be across there.

Are you envious of her ability to deal with death so easily?

Yes, and I'm not normally a jealous person by nature. She has just such complete faith. Death is the one thing that is hard for me. As you get older, you lose so many people who are important to you. I still miss my mother terribly and she died over fourteen years ago. I miss my husband. I miss his affection and being first with somebody. He would do everything for me. My brother has died, and friends are dying right and left. It must be nice to be able to accept it all as Jacqueline does, believing spiritually that they're all up there with the Lord.

But I just don't believe in all this about life after death. I

*not her real name

141

think when you're dead, you're dead. Dead, dead, dead. Your body goes to dust, if it hadn't already been burned to ashes.

When I think of my mother, I do wonder where all of that love has gone. We were such good friends and I saw her all the time. I miss her terribly. There's nothing as pure as a mother's love, no selfishness in it usually. Perhaps that kind of love dissipates after a person dies. Then it's gone. It can't reach me. I don't feel it coming through. I shouldn't say that though because...I just shouldn't say that...because who knows, who knows...

I had a cousin who was a very independent thinker. A number of years ago we talked about the afterlife ~ whatever happens to you after you die. She explained it so well. She said our spirit or soul is made up of some form of electricity. And when we die, it leaves our body and goes on up into the sky and just mingles with all of the other electrical currents in the air, and we just become part of the cosmos. This makes sense to me. Perhaps my mother and my husband are electricity out in the cosmos now.

Hmm...that's an interesting concept.

I know many people, especially Catholics, who pray a lot. They believe that if someone is sick and everyone prays for them, that will make that person well. Sometimes there are pray-ins or people have prayer lists. And if someone is very sick, occasionally the person does get well. Miracles just happen. I don't think that prayer makes the difference, but if some people think so ~ marvelous. But I just don't do it. But I guess if I were sick, I'd love to have them pray for me. Can't hurt. That's the way I look at it.

But I haven't thought about all of this as much as I should. I did come from a very religious family on both sides. My family was Presbyterian. So I've been exposed to this all my life. But I just don't think that God exists.

So I wouldn't really bother with this phone number. I wouldn't bother Her. I wouldn't bother It. I don't know what It is, whether It's male, female, neuter or nothing. And there are too many people to whom it would mean a lot more than to me.

✧

This interview with Isabelle was quite entertaining. I had to stifle giggles at certain points just to prevent my distracting her. Listening to the tape of our conversation again made me laugh out loud.

It was interesting to me that she did not think that she needed God but the poorer people did. And yet her friend, Jacqueline, who was rather affluent, did have a deep relationship with God.

I was intrigued with Isabelle's theory about the love turning into electricity in the universe. Perhaps there is a certain wavelength that resonates in unique ways around people who embody a deep love and that this wavelength never dissipates but continues to circulate. I would like to think that this might be true and that it might touch me at times. I know that I always feel attracted to people with big hearts. Some of the men whom I have been most attracted to were men with wonderful, upbeat personalities and big hearts.

Perhaps I give some of this love off when I'm in a deeply positive place. I can remember several instances when I was in a particularly happy, positive place emotionally, and total strangers such as shopkeepers were especially friendly to me, commenting on my "good energy." I do think there is far more to what makes up our soul-bodies than a frequency of electricity, though. But I could not say what that was.

When Isabelle talked about believing in nature but not God, I had to contemplate this. Could it be that the divine force within all of us, within all the atoms that we are made up of, puts forth a will to live and heal and evolve? I have a group of friends, and we joke about how our "work" is to "grow, change and evolve." Is this not the "mission" of all life on Earth?

There certainly is a powerful phenomenon in nature that pushes it to always heal or change. Volcanoes become mountains covered with forests over time. Abandoned parking lots sprout grass and trees. If we left them long enough, these lots would transition into forests full of biodiversity. I believe that people have a deep, innate drive to heal also.

When I give talks about current environmental trends and the need to be more sustainable, I discuss evolution and how we could interpret it as the Earth's having a greater intention to evolve to a place of greater complexity and biodiversity. But I truly believe that there is a divine force sourced from God that propels this.

✧

baltimore, maryland
october 1996

dear God...

it's me again.

i am struggling so with what to do with my life...i've been back from Omega for almost two months and i am so confused. i want to finish this book and yet need to get a job. i feel so torn. i've got some gardening clients but it is all i can do to get out of bed at times.

this afternoon, as i chopped tomatoes and dropped them into the pot to simmer down for sauce, i heard this voice bubble up in me: "i am a woman of the Earth." yes, it felt so right to be making tomato sauce. it is fall and this is the season to put up provisions.

God, i need help. support. sometimes i feel so full of courage and other times i am so terrified to write, to get out there, to live my life. i need to create a spiritual practice with discipline, and love myself in this. i want to feel the presence of the divine more. there were days when i really felt You when i was working in the gardens at Omega, but i want to feel this more. i want to learn to silence my doubts, the voices that say, "i cannot do this or that." i need to remember to be tender, be gentle, allow myself to feel it all. and walk through my fears. there are moments when i can, but it always feels like one step forward and two steps back. i guess that is progress, but this is so hard.

several nights ago, i was in so much emotional pain. it was a bad spell. i think You were there. i had collapsed onto my couch just sobbing and sobbing. i don't know where the pain came from, but it wouldn't stop. then i heard the sweetest happiest voices. they were so soft. they were calling to me through a misty veil that i could see, in my minds eye. "Come over and dance. Come over and play with us..." they were so full of joy. i sat there crying, wishing that i knew how to be with them, how to get through that veil. i responded, "i can't. i don't know how to get over there." they were the gentlest most joyful little beings. i don't know what they were. angels? Your little messengers?

God, did you send them to let me know that all i need to do is find the seams to slip through the veil? i so want to find my way through this confusion...

i give You my humble love,
Your daughter,

mare

CHAPTER 15

IS GOD IN CHARGE?

RACHEL COLLINS*
AGE: 43

YOU ARE A CHILD OF THE UNIVERSE,
NO LESS THAN THE TREES AND THE STARS;
YOU HAVE A RIGHT TO BE HERE.
AND WHETHER OR NOT IT IS CLEAR TO YOU,
NO DOUBT THE UNIVERSE
IS UNFOLDING AS IT SHOULD.

~ DESIDERATA (MAX EHRMANN)

In September of 1996, a woman named Rachel Collins called me for some gardening work. Rachel had gotten behind in the weeds in her family's small backyard in a borderline middle-class/blue-collar neighborhood. She couldn't afford to pay me, but she was willing to barter with a massage. So I agreed and promptly took care of her garden. Several weeks later she found time to give me an evening massage.

Fair-skinned with reddish hair and a trim figure, Rachel was a "supermom." I don't know how she juggled it all. She and her husband had two boys, age nine and eleven. Rachel worked about forty-five hours per week as a social

---

*not her real name

worker, gave five or six massages a week and, on top of that, had individual clients for counseling and still managed to run a household. I think it was all her family could do to find time to get to the grocery store to buy food for the week.

I liked Rachel from the moment we met ~ much as our lives were worlds apart. She was a married, suburban working mother with a lot of energy who loved to talk, while I was single and eclectic with a career that was hard to track. She was fascinated with my bohemian lifestyle since her life was so mainstream and fast-paced. When I mentioned my book, she asked me question after question about it, to the point I knew that I had to ask her if she wanted to be interviewed. Of course she said, "yes," although it took her about two months to find the time to do it. Finally she came over to my apartment on a Friday evening in late November so that we could talk.

✧

If I gave you God's phone number, what would you do with it?

I'd certainly have to call at my first opportunity. I'd have a lot of questions to ask.

First I would ask God: "Did You include all the technology that we use today in Your great plan?" Life-support machines that keep little babies alive who are neurologically impaired. Computer systems that put people out of jobs. Phone mail systems that are impossible for elderly people to figure out. Did God know that all of this was going to happen, and is He really overseeing it? Would He have wanted us to use all this technology?

I would also ask if He knew that our technology would destroy His creation as it has. The chemical waste discharged from factories and nearby children are born autistic. And all the cancer that is here. We can send people to the moon and build bridges, but we can't solve these problems. We can't control the pain that society struggles with every day in this world. Is all that part of His reality?

Or did He make the world up to a certain point and then let mankind's intelligence take over?

That's a big question. What do think God would say back to you if you asked Him that?

I think God would say that His reality was bigger and vaster than mine and that it would be hard for me to understand it all because I am thinking how a human being would think and not how He would think. He would tell me that my question was very valid, though.

I would want to know whether He really did know and plan for the Holocaust or the Vietnam War or the Israeli-Arab conflict all these years. Did He make the Ted Bundys of the world? Or is that somebody else's influence, like Satan, who creates all the bad things in the world such as people's selfishness? Is that really a part of sin, or is there something that we're all supposed to learn from this? And how do we survive it?

Would your question to Him be how to survive it?

How are people selected to survive it? Some people do, some people don't. I could go to Israel and be killed tomorrow. Or I could go to Israel and come back safe.

Is there even a selection process? Is it fate? Is He in charge of it? Does He really know every single thought, desire and detail of everybody's life and have it totally in control, as we are taught? I was told that He's in charge of every situation, every little minute thing, every time we stop and delay getting into a car. Is He really like this giant computer that knows every minute, every day, what every single person is doing?

So you'd want to ask Him if He is the one really running all this, or is there some other force?

Well, I know that if you believe in Christianity, you give your life over to Him for control. You believe you're a sinner and you need Him. But why couldn't He just make people good? If Heaven's going to be good, why do we have to wait so long and hurt so much in the meantime?

But again, I don't think He'd have an answer for me. Only that He's thinking something way beyond my understanding. I just have a pea-sized brain compared with His God-sized intelligence.

Is there anything else that you'd want to ask Him?

I guess I'd want to know if the Bible really tells how we got here and how to live. The seven days of Creation and the rules about marriage and the Ten Commandments. Are people supposed to stay married, as it says in the Bible? If so, why is it that fifty percent of all marriages don't make it? People are so blissfully naïve and get into relationships that don't work.

How much are we supposed to really understand about the human psyche and why people do what they do? I mean, the world is such a difficult place to just be, especially for children growing up in the slums. Is there any place where you can have peace and love and safety and nurturing? When people move to the mountains, do they really find that?

That is an interesting question you're raising ~ is there really a place to go for a better way to live?

Yes. Or do we have to do what is straightforward? Seek

Him. Seek to give our lives over and acknowledge that He's in control. People find happiness that way a lot. People will say, "God told me" or "God let me do such and such."

I would want to ask: "God, do you really talk to people and tell them what to do?"

Some people say that they have heard Him speak to them?

Oh, yeah. It happens. But I think that it's a personal thing. Some people believe that God says if you believe in Him, you should have lots of children. I think that kind of belief is a little strange, but if that works for some people, it's not for me to judge it.

I just can't believe that God wouldn't want me to think for myself, though. I know there are some people who think that all their thoughts come from God. Then there's a continuum of people who think it happens part of the time or none. You could probably put all kinds of religions along that continuum, too.

Hmmm...Do you have moments when you feel like God has talked to you?

Oh, I do. But not that He tells me what to think or feel. I think that God's definitely in charge of my life and sets up circumstances every day. For example, I just switched jobs because things were getting really horrendous at my old job. I got the new job over incredible odds. I know He put it there for me. There are just too many circumstances that led to my getting this job.

My old job was getting really terrible. There was a new administrator hired last year, and he started firing people right and left. It was just chaos. I don't understand why we all had to go through that unless we were all supposed to learn some deep lessons. But my self-esteem just got shattered through the whole experience, and I can't imagine what the usefulness of that was.　　.

Generally when people lose a leg or a loved one dies, I'll explain it by thinking that this taught somebody something or this helped people get closer to God. But if that's really true, it sure sounds like an awful way to have to do it.

But do you feel like this experience has helped you get closer to God?

No, because I don't do a whole lot of reflecting like that. I need to work harder on that. But I definitely feel like it has encouraged me to look at other experiences differently. We've signed up to do a missionary trip to Costa Rica now. I was vacillating before, but now I see it as a way to experience God in a different way, the same reason I went to Israel when I was in my early twenties.

I went to Israel to get in touch with my Jewish roots. I used to think that it was really hard that I lost my father. My father was Jewish, and he died when I was five. My mother had converted to Judaism before she married him, and she continued to raise us as Jews. But it was very hard after my father died. There were three kids in the family, and my mother was really cold and unnurturing because she was so stressed out.

Do you feel like that was God's path for you?

I don't feel that it was. I don't understand why my family would have to grow up without a father and why we would have to be under such stress. It was really horrible at times.

I know that it's probably nothing compared to kids who are sexually abused or women being raped or marrying someone who beat you. Some people have experienced some real trauma. In some ways I feel fortunate.

But my mother was really mean. People made a lot of excuses for her because of my father's death. Everything became about his death. I think that the world allows that kind of thing too much. People don't take responsibility for their behavior enough, and they're always blaming someone else. We have all these lawsuits because of this. I do wonder about whether this is all part of God's plan. Someone gets several million dollars as a settlement because someone else spills coffee on their lap. This is happening all the time now.

Oh, I do have another question. I get so tired of the fighting between races and religions. Why can't there be peace in religions? Why can't blacks and whites live together in harmony? Why can't people just look at others for who they are and just forget about what color that person is?

But again, I think God's going to say, "It's going to be crystal clear one day. You're going to know all the answers to this and you're going to understand." I think when the world ends and we all go up to this so-called Heaven, then we're going to understand a lot. We'll have a whole different way of thinking, not with a human type of brain. I still can ask "why?" and not understand it now, though.

What do you mean "when the world ends"?

When the whole world ends as it is prophesied. It might well end before I die. The rapture. Then we'll know. Then I'll probably even understand what is meant by Hell. I really do not believe in Hell even though it's in the Bible. I can't fathom that God would ever send anybody there, and nothing will convince me of that. So I figure I'll understand that better, too.

I know a lot of people think that these are dramatic times

we live in right now.

Yes, if we really got back to the family and religion, things would be a lot different. But everything is rush, rush, rush now. There are times I wake up in the morning and just pray to God to help me make it through the day. But we've got to pay the bills.

I think the whole basis is the Golden Rule ~ "Do unto others as you would have them do unto you." And that's just so lost and it's now ~ "Do for yourself, whatever it takes."

I worry about my kids. I worry about their self-esteem even though they get many more "I love you's" than I did as a kid. I mean, these are very warm, loving kids who know they are valued every day. They are compassionate kids who are good at expressing themselves. But I'd love to keep them out of all the struggles out there. The world's a hard place to raise children.

We've really taught our kids how to be givers. But think about it: how many people really give indiscriminately? Some people don't even know the joy of giving. They only know the pleasure of taking. They've just always been takers, and whether they've been taught that or it was modeled, I don't know. I think the bigger question is why are people made the way they are?

Good question. Rachel, can you tell me whether you attended church as a child?

We went to synagogue pretty often as kids, but nobody stayed active in it once we grew up. My brothers were bar mitzvahed, and I went through confirmation.

I'm still Jewish. I just don't practice. I practice Christianity. Being Jewish is something that you are, and a faith is what you practice. I believe that the Jews don't know that Jesus is God yet, but they'll figure that out eventually because it's prophesied that that will happen. There are more Christian Jews these days. "Completed Jews" is what they call them. I don't really associate myself with any group. I just really believe I know the truth and, in time, God will reveal that to Jewish people. My family attends a small non-denominational Christian church now.

That's great...Is there anything else?

I think the big thing would be why are kids abused? Every day I work with kids who are abused. Why does this have to happen? They go into foster care and then back to their parents and more abuse takes place. It happens over and over again. It's almost better if the parents die, so the kids can grieve and get over it and bond with foster parents. But abuse of kids is just about the worst. Emotional, physical, sexual ~ what are we supposed to learn from it? I can't come up with any answer for that.

✧

Rachel overwhelmed me with all of her questions, especially in comparison with some of the other people I had interviewed. I could not help but think that her mind raced as fast as her life, if not faster. But her questions were good and truly sincere.

She raised the question of how much God controls our life, stating that she thinks God wants her to think for herself as opposed to His giving her all of her thoughts. Yet some people believe that all their thoughts come from God. It would scare me to think that. Suppose I felt really angry with someone and I imagined some way to hurt him or her but did not act on it. I can't believe that God would put the negative thought in my head.

My instincts are a different thing, however. And they always guide me to a more positive place when I listen to them. Perhaps my instincts are connected to that God-place, that Divine part of me. We always have the volition to follow our instincts or not. But I don't believe God is telling us on an individual basis what to do or not.

I did find it interesting that Rachel selectively thought that God created circumstances for her, such as the new job, but that it could not have been His work for her father to die young. Just as I believe that our soul agrees to certain life work, I think our soul chooses our parents and our childhood experiences. I have heard a number of spiritual teachers say this, and it makes sense to me. Perhaps Rachel's soul chose a family in which her father dies young. Perhaps part of her life experience is to come to positive terms with that as she gets older. I have come to believe that we choose the lessons that we are born into.

One other statement that Rachel made was about a major condition of Christianity: that you give your life over to God and believe that you are a sinner. The concept that we were all born sinners always makes me shudder. I have a difficult time embracing that.

I'd rather believe that we come into the world with God's blessing and love. We do not come as marred humans who are touched with sin before we've even taken a breath. What a phenomenal awakening it would be if everyone were taught that our birthright is love and blessings from God as opposed to the negative teaching that we're already bad from Day One. Matthew Fox, a brilliant, former Catholic Priest who became a bit too radical for the Catholic Church and is now an Episcopalian priest, uses the term Original Blessing, and I love the connotations of that. I cannot help but wonder if the original sin concept that is promulgated throughout many Christian churches is just another means to control and disempower people.

Rachel also mentioned the prophecy of the world ending. I was surprised at how calm she was in saying that it could end before she dies. I guess there are many people who believe in the Apocalypse. Perhaps these people are so calm because they feel confident that they will find peace in life everlasting, as many are taught and as I was taught in the Catholic Church.

From what I've learned, there is a good chance that there will be some dramatic Earth changes, and perhaps large numbers of people will die but not everyone. That chapter in Earth's history has yet to be written, but with all the environmental changes under way and current war efforts, there have to be some repercussions. But I don't believe the world is going to end. Perhaps the world as we know it will end, though.

CHAPTER 16

BE A GOOD ONE

CHARLIE O'CONNOR*
AGE: 44

THE DAY WILL COME WHEN, AFTER HARNESSING SPACE,

THE WINDS, THE TIDES, AND GRAVITATION,

WE SHALL HARNESS FOR GOD THE ENERGIES OF LOVE.

AND ON THAT DAY, FOR THE SECOND TIME

IN THE HISTORY OF THE WORLD,

WE SHALL HAVE DISCOVERED FIRE.

~ TIELHARD DE CHARDIN

In December of 1995, I went to a large winter solstice party on the outskirts of Baltimore with a friend. A popular yoga instructor hosted the party, so there were many people attending who were interested in alternative health and spirituality. I met a couple who, it turned out, went to the same Catholic Church as my brother. We chatted for a bit and Charlie, the husband, explained that he did medical research at the University of Maryland, and Cathy, his wife, said she was a social worker. Of the two, Charlie was the more gregarious one. I told them that I was working on this book, and Charlie was immediately interested in being interviewed.

Unfortunately I lost Charlie's number when I got home, and time passed. In the interim I went up to the Omega Institute and returned. In mid-fall of 1996 I was invited to

*not his real name

participate in a Native American sweat in Baltimore County. Eager to get out and meet new people, I attended the sweat.

Shortly after I arrived, I recognized Charlie's blonde hair and short frame across the raging fire that was heating the rocks for the sweat. He was laughing and making jokes as he helped to tend it. To my surprise, with him was Father Paul, the priest from my brother's church. I had met Father Paul several months before when he presided over my brother's marriage and was shocked to see him there. I had never heard of a Catholic priest's participating in a Native American sweat. I walked around the fire circle and introduced myself to Charlie and Father Paul again.

Charlie explained that he had been telling Father Paul about sweats for several years, but this was the first one that the priest had been able to find time for. I was impressed that a Catholic priest would be open to such an experience. My perspective on Catholic priests was that they were too rigid to venture much beyond the folds of Catholic traditions. But then again, Father Paul was a fun, adventuresome kind of priest and clearly open to experiencing other spiritual traditions, as I learned. Later in the evening, he actually helped bring the hot rocks into the cramped sweat lodge and joked about how he was wrong in thinking that his "altar boy days were done."

Charlie asked me about my book again and one more time mentioned his interest in being interviewed. I was definitely still working on it and knew that an interview with him would be interesting since he was so sincere and intelligent, not to mention funny. So we scheduled an evening the following week for us to do it.

We held the interview at my apartment since Charlie had a three-year-old son and he knew that it would be very challenging for us to have an uninterrupted span of time to talk at his house. So we talked in my cramped little living room.

✧

If I gave you God's phone number, what would you do with it?

It's interesting. Since we ran into each other again last weekend and you told me again about the question that you ask people, what came to mind was an episode from the TV show recorded here in Baltimore, "Homicide, Life in the Street." It's actually a very powerful TV show that Cathy and I enjoy watching because the characters in it are struggling to find the goodness, the Godness, in their world.

One of the characters is an African American detective who has a really cynical outlook on life. He was educated by the Jesuits and he's obviously Catholic. In this one episode there are a series of murders where people are ending up in Dumpsters behind Catholic churches in East Baltimore. [Laughs]

Only Catholic churches?

Yeah, only Catholic churches. [Laughs] At the end of the show, they show the detective holding his head in his hands looking really upset sitting on the steps of a Catholic church. They caught the murderer but the woman has a mental illness and he knows she will be out on the street in no time. He knows she was conscious of what she was doing, but he could see that she was going to use her mental illness to manipulate her way out of paying for it. He's also struggling with his relationship with the Catholic Church.

A nun comes by and starts talking with him. He asks her, "How can there be a God? I don't see God anywhere." The nun responds, "Do you have a wife?" He says, "Yes, I have a wife." She asks, "Do you love her?" He replies, "Yes, I love her very much." The nun then gently says, "So then you know God."

Wow. That's very powerful.

So I recorded that one episode, and I play it once in a while. [Laughs] I see that as a strong message about God.

But anyway, back to the phone business. Probably the first thing to come out of my mouth to God would be, "Where are You during all of the horrors of the world? These TV shows dramatize horrors that happen in reality. Where are You in Rwanda? Where are You in Serbia? Where were You during the death camps? In the killing fields? In 'Nam? Korea, World War I? Were You in all that? How does all of that innocent pain factor into the plan?"

So, imagining that God would respond to you, what kind of response do you think God would give to that question?

Hopefully it would be all-illuminating. He might say, "Ah, you forget, I gave you free will." [Laughs] "You know you were given free will. And what you're seeing is the abuse of free will and the result of unconscious, unaware choices that people make and the types of evil and destruction that they wreak." That's what He might say. But what do I know about God?

That's true. What do any of us really know?

We can just try to use whatever we have to try to sense what God is. Everybody struggles with this, and their struggles are all different. Even if someone may have arrived there like a mystic, no two mystics have the same view. It's all different, and I think they all are right.

I would have other questions, too, like: "How did this

universe come to be? Did You really have anything to do with that? Are You part of that or are You before that?" You know God could have been created as part of Creation. [Laughs]

Another question could be: "Are You a He or a She?" Although I don't think I would ask that question because I think that God is beyond gender. We just use the concepts of male or female because we're attached to them. The traditional view is of this male figure up there, but I think that is due to our male-dominated culture. There's even the female image of God as Wisdom called Sophia in some belief systems. I think that God would have both male and female characteristics.

Maybe what we would see is what our minds tell us to see. Maybe the Pope would see God as a man, a Zeus type of person. Maybe someone else, like Matthew Fox or Julian of Norwich, a woman mystic from England, would see It as a woman.

[Pause]

I guess I'd wonder if there is truly life after death, or do we just disappear when we lose consciousness and the only thing that persists is people's memory of us? Is that what really happens? I'd certainly like to have the questions answered in my mind before the time comes.

You hear the New Age people say that you get reborn into a cat or another person. [Laughs] "Oh, I was a warrior prince at one time." Or something like that! [More laughter] Other images are that you move on to another plane of existence. I like that!

So you prefer that one. Maybe you're given a choice! (Laughs)

Yeah, maybe I am. I'd have to ask Him that.

I'd also ask Him about the whole idea of prophets. "Were You Jesus? Were You Buddha? Was that You in

Mohammed?"

What do you think He'd say to that question?

He'd probably say, "I just came down to be with you and try to teach you some things."

Maybe if God hadn't come down, it'd be a real mess! I don't know. The Old Testament is filled with stories that talk about God's appearance. The burning bush, the whole Exodus story ~ they really seemed to have happened. But did they really happen, or did someone just create these stories in a book?

What do you think God would say to that? (Laugh) Big questions!

[Hearty laugh] I don't know! He could say several things. He could say those are the products of some very active imaginations at the time. Or He might say, "That's pretty much what happened. I came to these people as Jesus and Buddha to show them a new way." Maybe God came down in a couple of other ways that we don't know about, too.

Then I'd ask, "Are you always there? I mean here, now! And if so, how do You do that? You're here and there's some nomad out in China and You're there, too! Based upon my sense of time and space, that's nuts!" [Laughs]

But according to what we're taught as Catholics, God takes on different dimensions in the form of the Trinity. There's God and then the God who walked on Earth two thousand years ago and then the God who's always present as Spirit or God's energy. So this Being manifests itself in many different ways.

I don't know.

Maybe if someone gave me that phone number, I might even find out that it is not a workable phone number. You know when you dial a number and the line says, "This number is no longer in service." Maybe that's what would happen.

It is a great fear of mine that there may be no God. I fear, in all my efforts to pursue a spiritual path to try to connect to God, that what I'm trying to do is to feed or comfort a psychological side of me that fears death and conjures all this up as a comfort to my mortality. That's something that I ask myself every once in a while.

Then I get to a place where the only way that I understand all this is by believing that there is something out there that makes this happen.

So that brings us back to the place where there is a God.

Yes. Recognizing the love that is there, in you. All that is here ~ love, creation. I'm talking not just about love but about companionship, friendship, relationship. When I say creation, I mean sunrises, sunsets, trees, mountain streams, even elves. [Laughs] My sense of God's presence is not just in the love I feel, but also in what is here.

It's a pretty amazing world that we live in. It's hard to imagine that it could just be here on its own.

Yeah. Another interesting question to ask God would be: "Are there other worlds around like this?" I think it would be folly for us to think that God's creativity was just limited to us. God may have many projects going on just like we have many projects that we do.

My hope is that He'd say, "Yes, there are other worlds, and let me show you! Let's go for a ride, just for a little bit. You won't even notice how much time has passed!" [Laughs] And I wouldn't be surprised if there were something wonderful going on out there. I just hope it's not like those types of critters that you see in sci-fi horror films like the Independence Day movie. Those are nasty. [More laughter]

[Pause]

But some people do harbor malicious intentions just like those nasty alien critters in the movies. It is because of people like Hitler that sometimes I do want to ask God, "Why did You give us a dark side, a shadow side? Why do we have thoughts of harming people and doing malice? What is the purpose behind that?"

Why do you personally think we have that in all of us?

I think it makes us struggle, makes us reach down into a place inside ourselves where we can say that this is what I should do. I think that if we didn't have that part of us tugging at ourselves, we wouldn't know what wrong was. We wouldn't have a sense of what loving or unloving behavior is.

I'm not sure if the world would be better off if everyone were completely loving all the time. Would writers be able to write? Would poets be able to compose poetry? Would painters be able to paint? If these creative people did not have to struggle, what would their efforts be like? Perhaps it would be easier for them to do their work, but whatever they created might be dull. It might lose some vitality.

I mean, who didn't struggle? Who didn't have to deal with the darkness? It's a part of life. Every force has an equal and opposite force. Buddha had to struggle underneath the tree. He had to come to grips with what he had to do in leaving his family, a wife, a child and all the different things that he was accustomed to. And the image of Jesus struggling in the desert with the dark side. Even he had a dark side that he had to work on.

I don't remember Jesus' dark side being a very big thing in the Bible.

Well, it's probably not brought out a lot, but it was brought out in the forty days and forty nights in the desert where he was tempted by his shadow and the Devil.

So why is that? I don't know. What good is it to have free will if you don't have options to choose from, to exercise that free will? The idea is to figure out the best choices ~ the right thing to do.

Would you have any questions to God about that?

About how do I decide about what is the right thing to do? Yes. "Give me a foolproof way of decision making!" [Laughing]

Although I imagine that He'll probably say something like, "Just look inside."

And that's probably what you do already. Hmmm...You mentioned the Devil a few moments ago, Christ went into the desert and met the Devil ~ is that something that...

You mean, does he really have a long pointy tail and horns? [Laughs] Well, does he?! [More laughter]

I guess it would be a good question to ask Him: "Is there another force out there like you that's in constant tension with you? Or is this part of the dark side of all of us that's just more pronounced in some people than in others?" And what is Hell? Is it really some place that you could go? What is Limbo? [Laughs] There's this place that people went to...

Do you mean purgatory?

No, there is another place ~ Limbo. It's not the dance. It was a place where babies who haven't been baptized went to, supposedly. And they had to hang out there until the next elevator got them. [Laughing] They taught us about it in Catholic school, one of the strange and interesting things that popped up sometimes. Someone brought it up again at a lecture on theology recently, laughing, "Remember Limbo? It just disappeared, and we never did find out where it did go. Did he just close up shop?"

I think Limbo was an idea that a theologian put out there that people grabbed hold of. A stupid idea ~ "Where do you put all the people who are not baptized but have not sinned? Oh, just create another motel for them." [Laughs] A way of having a complete order. Bad people went to Hell. Good people went to Heaven. Unbaptized people went to Limbo ~ they wait for the Second Coming.

That's another good question. "What is this Second Coming business?" Are we talking about a real physical coming where you have these Hieronymous Bosch-type scenes with lots of people writhing in dense crowds on the ground? He actually painted something called The Last Judgment or something like that. Very hellish-looking scene. I remember looking at that in a book when I was a kid and thinking, "God, that's weird."

So is this Second Coming going to be a big thing that's going to occur? Or are we talking about being in touch with the God, the Christ that's within us? I have a tape by this rabbi about the next coming of the Messiah. But if you are truly connected to God, you know here [pointing to his chest] that He is in here already.

So I just wonder if that's what they're talking about when you read those things. They're not talking about some event that you buy tickets for and the mountains fall. [Laughs] They're talking about a time when we all have a very personal, deeply spiritual type of awareness that we know Him again, fully, within ourselves.

Hmmm...Anything else?

I guess I've got some curiosity about the historical Christ. Every time I read a story, I wonder, "Gee, could that be right? How could that be?" [Laughs]

For instance, did he really raise Lazarus from the dead? That guy was nearly three days dead! And did he really put the ear back on the centurion after Simon Peter had cut the ear off one of the guards when they came for Christ in the garden?

But if I did ask God these questions, I think He might say back to me, "Do you really need to know that to know Me?"

And what would you say back to Him?

I would say, "No, I shouldn't. Why do I need miracles to know that You live?"

Although I have to admit, it would be nice to see these very tangible, outward signs. They would be so easy to grasp. For most of God's signs we have to go inside. It's a lot harder to do that.

It's interesting. We have a stigmatic here in Baltimore. I don't know much about her except what people have told me. Someone showed me pictures of her at a Mass out in western Maryland, and she was praying with her hands near her forehead in one picture, and in another there was blood running down from her forehead. I have a lot of skepticism about this. But, you know, I don't know! She could have had a capsule in her hand. But she might not. That's the type of miracle I'm talking about where some people have these tremendous signs.

But you could go seek her out if you wanted to, if she's right here in Baltimore.

Yeah, I know. And the next time something like this happens, I might. But do I need that to affirm God's

IF I GAVE YOU GOD'S PHONE NUMBER....

presence? I don't think I do. But I am curious. I'd like to check it out. Part of me is skeptical, but I'm willing to give things a chance.

People who channel are very popular right now, and I went over to a friend's house to watch a video of a beautiful blonde woman ~ they're always beautiful blonde women; that always makes me worry. Anyway, the woman is channeling someone called Rampha and she sits in front of an audience and starts making a very deep sound in her throat. And I thought, "Oh, I could have done that." There was nothing there to convince me.

There was no message, nothing other than a deep rumble in her throat?

No, it was just about how she can channel these other beings. You can see how I get real skeptical about those things. But I know that I don't really have a need for them in my spiritual life. I do wonder about these miracles, and it would be a good question for God.

Anything else that you'd like to ask? We've run a rather broad gamut of questions here.

Yeah, I might say, "Can I call you again if I have any more questions?" [Big laugh] "I've kind of run out of them right now. Are you going to be at this number later?" [More big laughs] "Or are you going to change it?"

So for you, you would just get on the phone and use this number and have a conversation. You would imagine something answering.

Sure, why can't you talk to God? My image of God is not of one who is intimidating and would put up a wall. I believe that God is Love. I feel that He would love to hear from me. [Laughs] He'd love to get my phone call.

I do feel that I talk to God sometimes, but I don't think that I do it enough. My spiritual practice is not what it should be or could be. Sometimes it goes along and then it sort of poops out for a while.

I used to try to spend a piece of each day in prayer or meditation. But that's very hard to do with a young child since I spend most of my time interacting with him and it's very hard to get off into a corner. A Carmelite nun helped me learn that prayer does not always mean going off alone to be still. There's a type of prayer that is just about how consciously you live your life, how you love your son. So I'm trying to have my actions be a prayer. Now that's not always achieved because of things going on, and sometimes you go nuts. [Laughs]

In the last couple of months, I've been trying to set aside time for prayer and reading and contemplating what the reading is about. The type of prayer that I do is called contemplative prayer where you keep quiet and repeat a mantra and try to block out other sounds. And I've been reading the Divine Office, which is a daily prayer of readings, psalms and Scriptures. It's been part of the Catholic Church for almost two thousand years, and some monks chant it every day, the whole cycle. I'm just making a little bit of headway into that.

It probably would be helpful to know a little bit of your background ~ so you were raised Catholic?

Yes, I was educated in Catholic schools all the way through college. My high school and college were run by the Christian Brothers. I've always considered myself Catholic. I was an altar boy and everything. And when I wandered away, it wasn't that I explored Hinduism or another belief system. I explored deviancy. Let's say I slept in on Sundays, often because I just crawled back in.

[Laughs]

My wife and I are still rather active Catholics. We're both on the parish council at our church. Our son will probably go to the church school next year. And occasionally I do sweat lodges. I don't see any conflict with that. It's all about God.

I just started a two-year program with the Diocese of Baltimore this fall. It's a program to teach you about Catholic tradition. We meet three times a month and it's pretty good. You meet all different kinds of people. Some people are really nuts. And other people have a progressive, liberal type of view.

Wonderful. You're really deep in your faith.

Well, yes, this is my lens to God. A year ago I heard a Tibetan monk on a radio show say, "It really doesn't matter what your religion is. It doesn't matter if you're Catholic, Hindu, Buddhist or Taoist, Shamanist, or whatever you are. Just be a good one, whatever you are!" And I took that to heart. I want to understand this lens to God as well as I can.

I'm working hard to gain knowledge about the Catholic faith, to better understand it so I can better discern where I am going to fit into this. Is there something for me to do here in the context of spiritual community?

Do you feel that you're getting more of an answer to that question ~ that there's something for you to do here?

I think that there's something for me to do. I'm just not sure what it is. I don't think that my professional scientific work is this. Perhaps it could be another dimension to me. But the things I do, the program I'm in ~ it's all trying to find that place inside me that's going to give me clear vision.

✧

Charlie O'Connor was a happy Catholic, and this was remarkable to me. This was a man who was emotionally healthy and knew how to experience joy. He laughed and joked throughout the whole interview.

I didn't think I had met more than five happy Catholics since I left the Catholic church. Unhappy Catholics, recovering Catholics, yes, but not happy ones. Of course it could be that I was not congregating where they were ~ in church. Instead, I was off searching for answers elsewhere.

There were several things that Charlie said that touched me. When he talked about Limbo and joked about how some theologian concocted the concept, I was impressed that he could forgive the Catholic church for this type of fabrication. It is my sense that there are numerous concepts that Catholic-theologians have created that are not in any way how the universe or God works. The Church's non-belief in reincarnation is only one. Yet it seemed Charlie was content to stay with the religion knowing these flaws. Perhaps he had a more forgiving nature than I do.

Charlie also talked about living life as a prayer. I loved how the nun helped him understand that his actions can be prayer, something that I aspire to achieving in my day-to-day life.

I love the idea of the Second Coming being a personal experience when most or all of us know God inside ourselves. When Charlie talked about this, I felt a deep warmth in my heart, as if opening my heart and having God there is just a choice, which I guess ~ it is. I much prefer to think about this type of Second Coming than an apocalyptic one.

What also impressed me about Charlie was that he expressed no judgements about other religions or spiritual paths. He was so open and admitted that Catholicism was the "lens" he was using but in no way implied that it was a better "lens" than any other. He was not going to try to convince me to come back to the Catholic church or follow his way as other people have tried to convince me. This made me respect him so much more. I imagine that his joy and enthusiasm for the Catholic church would do more to attract others to the church than many other people whose sole intent is to do missionary work ~ much as his words were not going to pull me back.

I cannot deny that a core part of me is Catholic and always will be. It was a powerful part of my childhood years and formed much of my sense of what is right and wrong. Certain positive aspects of the Catholic/Christian teachings, such as never stealing or lying, being kind to others ~ a large part of my integrity comes from this. But I feel too strongly that the Church has suppressed the feminine aspects of spirituality, not to mention encouraged a mechanistic view of the natural world as opposed to recognizing the overall consciousness and mystery of Earth Mother ~ that I could never go back.

CHAPTER 17

BREATHING GOD

Eden Gibson*
Age: 18

BECOMING A BUDDHA BY BREATHING IS ONLY
A BY-PRODUCT OF BREATHING. THE MOST
IMPORTANT PURPOSE OF BREATHING IS TO BREATHE
AND ENJOY BREATHING.

~ THICH NHAT HANH

Shortly after I returned to Baltimore in 1995, I met a divorced mother of three named Barbara Gibson in a spirituality/healing class based on Rebirthing◆. Barbara was assisting in teaching the class. She and I immediately hit it off with our common interests in alternative health and gardening, so a deep friendship developed in spite of the fact that I was single with no children and she had three.

I also got to know Barbara's children well. Eden was the oldest at eighteen. Next was Brian at fourteen, and the youngest was Kendra at twelve. The whole family, including her ex-husband, was active in an informal spiritual community led by the same person who taught the Rebirthing class.

Barbara's ex-husband was rather wealthy and thus she could afford to be an at-home mom with her children even

---

*not her real name
◆Rebirthing is currently known as Integrative Breathing. The name was changed in 1999 to better
convey the broader healing potential of the breathing work.

as they reached high school age. All of the children went to a private Waldorf School during elementary and middle school. (The Waldorf educational system incorporates spiritual development into the curriculum along with other standard academic work.) After Eden graduated from the Waldorf School, she enrolled in a public high school but had a difficult time during her freshman year, so Barbara chose to homeschool her for the remainder of her high school years.

Eden had always struck me as one of those incredibly "together" young people. I have met a number of these individuals who are young chronologically but wise beyond their years. She was tall and lanky and beautiful both on the inside and out. Since I had first met her, she cut her beautiful, thick brown hair from a long ponytail to a close-cropped look. The shorter hair brought out her high cheekbones and big brown eyes even more. She had a very gentle "old" presence and it was a pleasure to be with her.

About two years after I first met Barbara, I invited Eden to join me for a hike. I had always enjoyed her company and she loved to be outdoors, so I thought it would be fun to have her as a hiking buddy. Her parents had sent her to a Native American camp for six summers, so she was very at ease in the woods. She had just completed her G.E.D. several months before and was taking a year off before college.

We got on the topic of my book, and she was quite intrigued by it. I asked her about doing an interview. She was very open to it so we set it up for the following week at my apartment.

Eden came over early. I made dinner for the two of us, and then we talked in my living room.

✧

If I gave you God's phone number, what would you do with it?

Well, I've been thinking about this. And I feel like being given God's telephone number would be like giving me my own phone number. I kind of believe that each of us is God. When I thought about calling God up on the phone, I had to wonder what I would ask. And I just realized that anything I would ask, I would be able to answer myself.

Perhaps I'd have questions that I wouldn't be able to answer, but they wouldn't be relevant to where I am in that moment.

Any real question or dilemma I've had throughout my life ~ I've been able to sort through on my own. It's been through my meditation and my knowing myself that I've been able to answer it. I strongly believe that we all have our own answers.

So if someone offered you this phone number to God, you might take it and yet be thinking that you really don't need it because it would be just like talking to yourself?

Kind of...I really believe we need to recognize the God within each of us. So this idea of a phone number to God ~ it's so bizarre to think of Him in that way.

I feel that God is more like an energy. I know that I'm young and inexperienced, but so far my sense of experiencing God is when I experience the energy flowing through me when I am being completely present to myself. I guess my most intimate experiences with God have been through the Rebirthing work I've done. There were times I felt like I was breathing God.

What do you mean by Rebirthing?

Rebirthing is an intense form of meditation where you're lying on the floor and breathing deeply but quickly. I did an eight-week course in it several years ago and have been going for Rebirthing sessions since. It's part of the spiritual community that my parents are involved in.

The quick breathing puts you in an altered state. My dad describes it as hyperventilating because you get so much oxygen into your brain. You can feel anything from intense anger to sobbing to bliss, but a lot of Rebirthing is about feeling energy in your body. Each session I've had has been very different. Some people have had past life experiences or just resolved issues that were deep in them. For instance, I had a really hard time dealing with my parents separating, and through Rebirthing, I released some of the pain from those experiences.

There have been times during a session when I felt like I was gasping with God. Every breath I took in, God was breathing out. As I breathed out, God was breathing in. My breathing felt like a connection to everything as if there were no separation between me and everything else. It was like I never ended and nothing else began. And God was all of it.

So I feel like I already have God's phone number. I feel like I already know how to reach God. My way to do this is to be completely present for myself. I do that in many ways. Sometimes it's with a Rebirthing session. Sometimes I play the piano and just completely let go of everything ~ of my thoughts and judgments. You know all that stuff that's in our head that's controlling us so much of the time. Letting the energy flow. It can happen by even taking a walk or meditating.

It almost sounds as though you've had some mystical experiences with some of the things you've done.

Well, even when I was a little girl and my parents were atheists at the time, I always believed in God. I thought it was wrong that they did not believe. I actually wanted them to send me to a Catholic school because I had friends who went there, and I used to go to church with them.

The wilderness camp that I went to for six summers opened up a great deal for me. I started being more conscious of the Earth and passionate about nature there. It was also there that I learned to be spiritual with God in nature. After those camp experiences, I thought I needed to be in nature to be with God, but after I learned the Rebirthing techniques, I realized that I could be with God wherever I was, even walking downtown in the middle of the city.

When you talk about being with God, have you ever felt that you've gotten messages back ~ that there has been any dialogue?

I have never had any experience of actually talking to God, not in that way, but I feel like I have talked to God in a different way. I felt like I was breathing God, like an exchange of consciousness. I feel like I've been connected to that place and been able to advise myself...

That place...What is that place?

It's a place of non-judgment and unconditional love, I guess. I've never really explained this before because it never seemed necessary. It never mattered to me exactly where it came from. But just that there's this place ~ someplace in my gut ~ where there's this wisdom, whether it's something I breathe in or...I don't know. It feels like a place of non-judgment and unconditional love that is advising the human part of me. I mean, to be human is to be judgmental. I'm going to be judgmental, there's no stopping it. It's just being aware of it and not letting that control me. I've learned this over and over.

Where did you learn this? Was it in your Rebirthing course?

I don't know. I guess I first learned about meditation at the wilderness camp that I went to. We each had a special medicine area in the woods where we would go for one hour each day. I learned to look at a stone or a stump for a long period of time and just let my thoughts float away.

I guess you could say I was trying to still my mind. At times it's harder to let go of my thoughts than other times. When I am playing the piano or going for a walk, it's not always so easy to let go of the chatter.

Finding that stillness can be very hard. But getting back to this phone number, would you just throw it away then, or...

No. I don't want it to sound like I wouldn't want to have an experience in God, because I want that more than anything. But I guess it's just a matter of just having it, you know? Having the connection to God.

I guess I get caught up in thinking that if I do something, then that means I will be more connected to God. Like if I make more money, I'll be happier. Same kind of thinking.

The telephone number and the act of calling God isn't really the issue, is it? It's really just an invitation to be present. I would take the telephone number itself and remember: "Okay, I have to be with God right now."

This reminds me of Thich Nhat Hanh [a Vietnamese Buddhist monk who is world-renowned for his teaching and writing on peace, love and compassion]. I went to a three-hour lecture that he did. Sporadically through the lecture, one of his monks would ring a bell as a reminder for us to remember to stop and be in the moment ~ be with God. That's how I would see the telephone number. It would be a reminder for me to stop and just be with God.

And it's certainly not like I'm at a point where I feel that I'm with God all day long yet. [Laughing] Sometimes not even at all for a week or a month. But Thich Nhat Hanh wrote in one of his books, I think it was *Peace is Every Step*, that not everyone can be in the monastery all day long. So the telephone ringing can be a mindful reminder to just stop and be with God.

Do you define being "mindful" and focusing on "being with God" as the same thing?

Yeah. Being mindful or being present. When I am fully present, I am fully present with God. I'm not at a point where I feel that all day long. But I'm trying. I keep prayer beads with me all the time, and if I feel like I'm being judgmental toward another person or myself at work, I'll remember the beads in my pocket and start to quietly say a prayer for each one on the string. It's so easy to make a mistake at work and beat myself up for it. But that's not going to resolve anything. So I need a reminder to be mindful, and the beads help.

When I've been really mindful, I've had experiences where I felt like a question or an answer really came from God. So I don't know if I feel like God is really separate. I feel so connected sometimes that I could not say if the answer came from me or God since I don't feel a separation those times. The answer comes through me to me.

Yes, and you are God. That's what you said initially.

Yeah, I don't really know enough about religion to really speculate on it, but it seems like there's a lot of focus on loving God unconditionally. And the real lesson is loving ourselves, as if we're God, you know? But, I mean, that's what religions are trying to get across. It's the same in

Buddhism, Judaism, all the religions. I kind of feel like this is my philosophy.

✧

It was such a joy to interview Eden. It astounds me still that she was only eighteen years old. She was so clear about her connection to God and lived so much in her higher self. I was in awe of her.

When I did the course with Barbara, Eden's mother, I tried some Rebirthing sessions but to no avail. I remember just breathing deep and hard and fast and having the Rebirther try to guide me in releasing whatever needed to be released. Each time all I felt was exhausted with little sense of relief once the session was over. I guess it's just another teaching that one person's path to find God is not necessarily another person's.

Eden's comment about how being human is to be judgmental was an interesting one. Perhaps she was speaking about how we generally see ourselves as separate from God and from each other; consequently, we create judgments about ourselves and each other. It is only when we come from a deep place of compassion and connection that we can shed the judgments to feel love instead. How I aspire to experience that most of the time. I think this is what she meant by being present to God or mindful. Being in that place necessitates shedding any sense of separateness.

I loved that Eden keeps prayer beads in her pocket to remind herself of where her thoughts are going. I confess that I am not that conscious. I let many a judgmental thought through without catching it. This is work for me.

Eden had such spiritual wisdom for a person her age. I truly wonder if she is one of those gentle souls who walks the Earth to teach the rest of us. It was an honor to interview her.

CHAPTER 18

LIP SERVICE

PAUL HORWITZ*

AGE: 48

WHILE GOD WAITS FOR HIS TEMPLE
TO BE BUILT OF LOVE, MEN BRING STONES.

~ RABINDRANATH TAGORE

In the summer of 1997, I took a two-week road trip to New England to visit various friends and relatives. One of my stops was at an aunt and uncle's in a nice, upper-middle-class neighborhood north of Boston.

I was visiting over the weekend, so my aunt decided to invite some of their close friends over for a barbeque. It was a fun, informal meal with three other couples, including Paul and Carole Horwitz. While we ate, I ended up sitting off to one side of the patio next to Paul, a tall, graying man in his late forties with a healthy paunch. Initially Paul intimidated me with his abrupt, almost gruff demeanor, but I soon discovered we shared some common liberal political views. He also told me a little about his engineering firm that worked on corporate building construction.

Of course the topic of my book came up, and he quietly shared with me that he did not talk about his spiritual beliefs, not even with his wife. Hearing this, I was intrigued and later asked him privately if he might be interested in

---

*not his real name

being interviewed. I assured him that he would be anonymous and coaxed him into agreeing. Paul definitely appeared to be one of those confident, tough men who did not reveal his vulnerable side often, so I was eager to see whether a more sensitive side of him might emerge in the course of the interview. Moreover, if he did not share his spiritual views even with his wife, it would be fascinating to find out what they were and if they were as controversial as he implied.

Paul finally said that he would do it. He suggested that we meet at his house the following day. He knew that his wife would be out doing errands with their teenage twin daughters in the mid-afternoon, and thus the house would be quiet at that time.

The Horwitzes lived in the same neighborhood as my aunt and uncle, so it was easy to find their house the next day. We talked in their nicely appointed den where beautiful family photos dotted the walls and mantelpiece.

As we started the interview, Paul told me more about himself. His family was Jewish, but he considered himself a cultural Jew, not a religious Jew. He had never been bar mitzvahed and made it his practice to stay away from synagogue. He and his wife were raising their daughters as cultural Jews.

✧

If I gave you God's phone number, what would you do with it?

Well, I don't think you'd have it. So I'd be skeptical. [Laughs] I wouldn't believe you if you told me you did have it. Carl Sagan touches on all this stuff in his book *Contact* and the movie by the same name ~ all these questions about God. I agree with most of what he says although I think he's more charitable in the book and film than what he really believes.

The way I look at it, I really don't know what the term God means since it's been so reviled with people doing horrible things in the name of God throughout the ages. I'm willing to believe in evolving science as we know it. But if somebody has to posit something beyond that, why go to the extent of creating the all-powerful concept of God? I just accept the fact that we don't understand what it's all about yet, and periodically we get greater understandings.

I don't see that you have to create this fairytale fiction of God, whatever that means, in order to lead a moral life and do right things. People say that if we don't have religion, then people will think anything's possible and they can do anything, kill anyone. I don't get that sort of concept.

So I would be very, very skeptical of some phone number. You must know that I'm very private about my beliefs because I'm certain that most Jewish people would take offense at them. But as far as I'm concerned, the Bible ought to be junked for about a thousand years and then looked at as a historical text. All this stuff about the Bible's being the Word of God and divine revelation. It drives me nuts! It's just a book that some people wrote, like any other book. There's some nice wisdom and some great poetry in there...

Have you read the Bible?

Oh, I've read much of it, sure ~ been forced to one way or another. [Laughs] But people just go nuts over it. And they are so ignorant about it. I bet if you walked down the street and asked most Americans what language the Bible was written in, most would say English, rather than Aramaic, Hebrew or whatever it was, Greek.

And a lot of the quotes, "God shall do this unto that..." blah, blah, blah. It's all fabrication. It's very nice fabrication, and there's certainly some wisdom and interesting precepts and some terrific writing in there. There's probably a lot of interesting historical text in there, too. But to raise it to the level that it's gotten is outrageous.

Then, getting back to a phone number, you'd....

Well...I guess I'd take it and call. I'm skeptical, but I wouldn't be so cynical or so presumptuous as to say I couldn't be wrong about all these things. But that presumes that God has a phone and some guy up there, or gal, is sitting around and is going to talk English to me and explain things in a way that I can understand. I just think that's a good fantasy.

Beyond what science offers us, I believe you can make your own decisions about how to lead your life. But I don't think you necessarily have to posit an outside thing such as God in order to justify your existence and to figure out what you want to do. For some reason, millions of people do need this, at least as I can understand what they're saying. I have no idea really what they're saying because I don't think I have the receptors for the message that they put out. It just goes right by me.

Maybe they need these beliefs to live. I don't need it. I'm perfectly happy. I think there is plenty of mystery and wonderment in everyday nature: a flower unfolding, the sun coming up, the diversity of life, reproduction. There's such richness in these things. It's overwhelmingly stimulating. There are more things to contemplate in these phenomena than I'm prone to contemplate anyway, so why do we have to have yet another thing beyond that? That's already plenty! [Laughs]

But that's not enough for most people. They have to invent God to explain it. Why don't they just enjoy all of this for what it is? It seems perfectly adequate to me.

So that still doesn't answer how it all got there, though. Do you personally have any theories on that?

Well, the creation of the universe is the ultimate question for a lot of people. I personally think the universe has always been here. But people invented the answer of God: "God created it." But why invent any answer? There's no need.

But if God did create the universe, then who made God? I mean, where did God come from? It's an imponderable, and you can spend only so much time pondering imponderables before it's time to move on. [Laughs]

Think about the Big Bang. Was God created in the Big Bang? You could go the route of asking whose finger touched the light that created the Big Bang. That begs the question of who created God again. "Well, God's infinite and always has been and always will be." Well, fine. Why don't we just eliminate God and say the universe was always infinite. By its own immutable laws, the universe is what we experience and try to figure out. So why do people need God? The universe is adequately challenging to understand in itself.

Sure, there will be things that science will never be able to explain. I'm comfortable with that. I just put them into the category of things that will never be explained. [Laughs] People can call it God if they want. But I still ask the question ~ what's God?

I really don't have any burning, compelling reason to endlessly focus on these things at this point in my life. I went through a phase when I did when I was younger and came to these conclusions, and they seem to be holding up for me so far and that's fine.

So you went through a phase of asking some big questions when you were younger?

Yeah, it was in the heyday of drug-induced hippiedom. I was in college in northern California. Great stuff. I can't talk about it much now because some people get hysterical, but it was real interesting.

I had a checkered college career. I actually spent the first two years of college hiking through the redwood forest on campus most of the time. My college campus was close to a good-size park with huge redwood trees and I just combed it. I had grown up in Brooklyn, New York, and it was not until college that I understood that there could be two trees growing next to each other without a sidewalk between them. I'd cut my classes and get high and take six-hour hikes a couple of days a week. I'd just hike and say, "Wow," and then sit there and look at nature and contemplate life. I was high most of the time.

I had some wonderfully cosmic experiences. The most incredible one... [Laughs] Marijuana was nice but LSD was the drug of choice. I took LSD as a very profound spiritual undertaking, not like "Hey, let's get fucked up."

One particular morning, around six, a couple of us went out into the forest for an LSD experience. We took the acid shortly after getting to one overlook. In little time, I was totally blown away. It was incredibly cosmic...Time standing still...Ego loss...If you'd asked me, I couldn't have told you my name or even articulate in English. My mind was just completely gone. But I could feel all my molecules vibrating. Everything was at a molecular level. I could feel my molecules completely blended into all the molecules of the redwood forest around me. I remember staring at a tree and just seeing it and hearing it vibrate... [He gesticulates, waving his arms above him, making a large humming sound.] It went through all these color changes. I just sat there. I have no idea for how long. I was recognizing that all my molecules were the same molecules as those in the cosmos and feeling a total oneness with it all. I could see that there was this interaction, and what I was putting out was coming back...I mean literally at the atomic level.

It was a very profound religious experience. But I didn't think about God. I just felt very cosmically at one with all the beings. I remember lying there on my back and feeling the entire curvature of the Earth and feeling the Earth moving through space. It actually seemed as if it was pushing me and I was holding it back, the same feeling you get of being pushed back into the seat when a car accelerates. I could feel the Earth's movement, and I was aware of the entire Earth and cosmos history at some level.

I had a few more experiences like that afterward but none as good as that one. Mystics write about the heavens opening, and perhaps my experience was similar. I've never had any cosmic experiences or feelings of oneness with the universe in normal life. It's only been in extreme states of psychedelic drug inducement. Sometimes I'm able to think back and relate to that experience in some way or another but only as I remember it.

In retrospect, I had what I felt was a substrate experience. That experience really defined how I feel about the universe. My molecules are the same as all the other molecules in the universe. And they happen to be constituted in the form that's me while that chair over there has molecules that happen to be constituted in that form.

In fact, there is new scientific evidence that shows that all our molecules are changed every seven years, all the atoms of our bodies.

Didn't Deepak Chopra write about that in Quantum Healing?

He may have. I just read about it in a recent article. But our atoms are always changing. If you go to the baseball game, you exchange atoms with every person in that stadium, fifty thousand people, in five minutes. The mixing at the atomic level is vastly more than anybody normally thinks about.

That's fascinating, but do you ever wonder about what makes you different from the chair over there? What allows you to think and have consciousness beyond your atoms and molecules ~ that some call the soul or the essence of who you are?

Nope, I never think about that. It's just the way it is. I don't think about the soul or essence, and I believe that when I die, it's over. Nothing else happens. That's the end of me. Period. My molecules will disperse back into the environment. I am a part of this cosmos, and I don't need to think about where I'm going to end up after I die. I'll be worm food. And glad of it. Stick me out in the front yard with a cherry tree on my navel. I'll be happy.

I don't believe that something flies out of me and goes to some great bus station waiting room for souls in the sky, waiting for its name to be called to be assigned to some badger or another person or ant. When I die, that's it.

Beliefs like life after death are all junk. They're just designed to make us feel better in some manner. Although I don't know what is the problem that you have to feel better about. But obviously billions of people in the world feel there is a problem. They seem to want to believe that they will last indefinitely in some manner or another. And they won't. That's what it's really about, right? Reincarnation or souls, these are all different ways of saying "I don't want to let go 'cause I need to continue..." And there's no empirical evidence that any of this ever happens, so we invent stories with ghosts and other mythic creatures to help explain it.

I think we all have our own inner demons that drive us to do things, but that's different. We invent all sorts of things that we blame for our actions or we conjure up for fantasy, such as space aliens and UFOs. They're pure imaginational products. As is Mickey Mouse...And the

Energizer Bunny and the great god Thor. They're all mythic. Which is fine ~ just don't let them control your lives or your actions, which is what most people seem to do.

So you would take this phone number and make the call?

Oh, sure, out of curiosity. I'd call. And if we could really have a conversation in English, I guess I'd ask a lot of questions: "So, what is the story of the Universe? And who are You and where did You come from? All these things that I've just described ~ am I correct? Or does everyone just design their own universe and whatever they design works for them? So, if I choose to believe in Barko the Dog God, then that's going to be my reality, and if somebody else believes in Jesus, then that's theirs or...What's the ultimate fate of mankind? Is there life on other planets?"

Those are the kinds of things I'd ask. I'd also ask, "Why are we having this conversation in English and what's your role in all these things?"

But I just can't take a phone number to God seriously. You call up and you get what sounds like some male, basso profundo voice on the other line [in a very deep voice], "Yes, Paul. This is God. Ask your three questions." I just don't think it works that way. Might as well be: "Okay, God, wave your magic wand."

My children know how I feel, and I think they probably agree with me on most of this. I was raised as a cultural Jew, not a religious one, so that is my background. As a family, we practice some cultural things from Judaism that we like, but that's it. Friday night and Saturday are always family time. We might go to the movies or go out to dinner, or go for a bike ride on Saturday. But we don't go to synagogue and pray because it just gives me the heebie-jeebies to do that.

My wife, Carole, does not agree with me on all of this.

She has a more religious...I don't know ~ you'd have to ask her. But she believes in reincarnation. We don't talk about this stuff very much because I usually end up teasing her. She gets frustrated with me.

So the two of you have very different beliefs.

Yes, so we rarely talk about it.

But there is something else about all of this. Religions have caused much of the mayhem and murder in world history, supposedly all for God. Whether it's the Protestants versus the Catholics, Muslims versus Jews or things perpetrated on indigenous cultures, vast amounts of killing and chaos and imposition have been done in the name of religion. It's all horrific.

Just the other day there was an article in the paper about Christian missionaries off somewhere in South America. Please! Give me a break! When all the Christians in the world have gotten their act together and can own up to their history of mass murder, then I think they ought to listen to other people for about another thousand years before they go off with their nonsense doing missionary work somewhere.

So, you're saying that you don't approve of the missionaries...

No...No, I don't. Of the world's various religions, Christianity has been one that has been particularly oriented toward brutalizing vast numbers of people, including themselves. I remember studying the French Protestant-Catholic wars in college. Whole cities of men, women and children were herded onto barges that were dragged out into the Atlantic Ocean and sunk. People drowned by the thousands.

Then there was the Spanish Inquisition! Just horrible

torturing and killing. This is religion? The Nazis weren't exactly Christian, but much of their racism came out of a dark side of the Christian ethos. It's only the Christians that have given smallpox blankets to the Brazilian Indians and let them die in vast numbers. That's what I see religion has been about and is about now. Sooner or later we have to stand up and say: "This is a lot of junk, and it's real bad, and we need to go in the other direction for quite some time before we can strike the balance."

In my opinion, all organized religions are made up of myths that people choose to believe in. I've always resented the fact that these things are presented as if they were fact. To me, the religious gods are as much mythic creatures as Mickey Mouse is. But no one is running around killing in the name of Mickey Mouse. But, in the name of Jesus Christ, that's what's gone on in the past and continues to go on now.

I really think we ought to own up, especially the profound proselytizers. I'm talking about Billy Graham or Jerry Falwell. But that does not happen in this culture.

And those proselytizers on the street...When those true believers approach me with that wild-eyed zealot look in their eye, it really scares me. Those are my least favorite kinds of people to be around. I backtrack furiously. [Laughs]

Do you think religions teach any wisdom?

Well, actions speak louder than words. If they do, I don't see the wisdom being translated into anything very often or very much. But I have seen that the body count is very high. That's what I look at.

What about someone like Mother Teresa?

She's a rare exception to the rule. As far as I know about

Mother Teresa, she does good deeds. But I don't know what kind of bunk you have to swallow to get treated in Mother Teresa's tent. Do people have to do something? Or do they just show up and be poor and she gives them care? If so, that's great. If that's her motivation, that's fine. But that's the rare side of it.

Look at Bosnia, Ireland, Sri Lanka, the Middle East, on and on and on...The hate groups in the United States. All these things done in the name of religion. So I don't see where the wonderful, good things of religion have come in. I personally would rather spend my time ignoring them. But in this culture you've got to give it some lip service, because that's the culture we're in, but I'm damned if I have to believe it.

A friend of mine is an elected official in the state legislature, and he's told me that they start with a prayer every day. They can't do it in the schools, but they pray to God every morning when the state government opens up. I think it's all real, real bad.

I didn't know they did that in government.

Yeah, they do. I really don't talk about this with most people. They would think that what I'm saying is weird and blasphemous. I'm obviously a minority. But it's what I really believe. So a phone number to God would just be part of the unvarnished gibberish that the rest of it is. Sure, I'd test it ~ out of curiosity. But that would be my only motivation.

Okay...Is there anything else that you would like to add?

[Pause]

I have to tell you that I am responding very literally to this question of a phone number to God. I'm thinking of God in the common parlance of the definition of God, and

I really have issue with that concept.

But if you're asking about my spiritual world view ~ that's different. I do believe that there are some cosmic forces out there. Some we have defined scientifically, like DNA or electricity or the speed of light, and some we have not. But there does seem to be some glue that makes everything happen, some great life force or energy force in things that extends throughout the cosmos. I'm sure there is more than just the scientific process at play here. Whether there is some greater intention behind it all, I have no idea.

From time to time I've experienced the mystery and wonder of it such as some cloud formations or a beautiful vista or even some kids doing something. But I think the mystery is something that you can't put into words and you just have to feel.

Playing catch with my girls is like that. It's a great spiritual experience for me. I love it. We've got the baseball mitts and balls. We go out and we play catch. That's as profound a spiritual experience for me as any other I have ever had. These are my offspring, and I feel the generational thing. I love them a lot and I like them a lot and they're fun to be with. I think about where they came from and how I am connected with them and the mystery of that. All of the great spiritual mysteries of life can be caught up for me in that experience. All the magic. And they feel it, too, because we've talked about it. It's one of those great family bonding things. I feel a lot of love then.

I get a lot of spiritual nourishment from being around close friends, too. I also feel it when I'm out getting a dose of pure nature.

It's interesting how you talk about all the love that you feel when you're playing catch with your daughters. Did you also feel a tremendous amount of love when you were having that LSD experience in the redwoods?

It could be that I felt love when I had that LSD experience in the redwoods, but it was very different. When I'm out playing catch with my daughters, I have a conscious awareness of what is going on. In the redwood forest, it was at some level of pure experience that I cannot describe. I had no conscious awareness. It was purely in just being there and the energy levels felt from the cosmos, the energy waves.

Sometimes when I hear people talk about God experiences, I wonder whether we are just experiencing the same thing but have chosen different words, and I react negatively to their words. Or are we talking about completely different things? I'm not sure. I tend to think we are thinking about really different things. I know that if they said that there was this mysterious life force that was undefinable and we won't lay any definitions or expectations on it, I'd feel more comfortable.

So, if someone gave me a phone number to the mysterious life force, I'd say, "Cool. Let's call." But if they said: "Paul, in the name of the mysterious life force, we have to put you in prison" ~ that's very different. I don't think that's the nature of this mysterious force. But I see people taking their understanding of It and imposing horrible things on other people in the name of It. So I just put this whole thing of God down.

Yeah, there's some cosmic mystery and excitement out there, a great deal of it. I experience it. I enjoy it. But I don't obsessively ponder it. And the times that I ponder it are fewer and further between. But it is, at times, the wellspring that I go back to.

✧

It is clear why Paul does not talk to people about his religious/spiritual beliefs. He was judgmental of all persons involved in any organized religion, especially Christianity. And yet he acknowledged a creative force within the universe that most of us refer to as God. He is the only person I have met (to my knowledge) who lumps the term God with the negative aspects of organized religion only and not with any positive attributes.

Some of his beliefs were very similar to another man's whom I interviewed. This other man spewed a litany of horrendous acts that the Catholic Church had perpetrated over time. The interview took place in the early phase of my book process, and I truly feared that if I wrote that interview up I'd be "tarred and feathered" in the modern-day sense. Ironically, the tape recorder had not been turned on properly and I had not recorded anything. The interview was lost, and I thought I was saved.

Perhaps it was not just coincidental that I found another person with similar beliefs. Maybe there are many intelligent, thinking people who are horrified by the history of Christianity, and finding two was rather easy.

I have to admit that I did not agree with Paul on whether religion teaches wisdom or not. I believe that organized religion does have the capacity to encourage people to be more wise and compassionate. Leaders of various faiths do motivate their congregations to look more deeply at how kind they are or accepting or forgiving.

The one thing that I take issue with, at least in the Catholic Church since that is what I know, is that people are not taught to set their boundaries with each other. I'm not sure if "turning the other cheek" is what Christ really meant. If a couple is married and one spouse is verbally abusive to an extreme, then the other spouse has every reason to try to set limits on their mate or end the relationship. It is important to communicate to others that some behaviors are intolerable and you will not accept it. It is a critical aspect of leading healthy lives. Somehow the Catholic church and perhaps other Christian faiths have missed an important teaching ~

that it is good to set limits on destructive behavior and stop it in whatever way is most positive. And because these faiths do not teach this, marriage for life sometimes evolves into hellacious relationships ~ for life.

Paul's belief that we die and there is nothing to us other than worm food for a cherry tree was mind-boggling for me. So much of how I see my life, or rather my evolution of the many lives that my soul has experienced, is that I'm on an infinitely long journey to evolve spiritually ~ to move closer and closer to the consciousness of the creative force/God in the Universe. I believe that there is a greater purpose to our living, and this is what motivates me to get out of bed in the morning and continue to give to others and work on myself to be a more compassionate, God-loving person.

✧

baltimore, maryland
march 2001

dear God...

i think i am growing and learning. earlier tonight i sat in front of my altar and lit the candle in the front and just let the angst of a tough day wash out of me.

thank you, Creator and Earth Mother, for all that You have brought into my life. i have been feeling more at peace these days, more contented and loving of myself and my choices. even when i sit down for a meal, i am aware of the Earth's love going into the food before me and my body taking in this gift.

i feel so settled here in baltimore. my environmental and gardening work has been going well, and i've been paying my bills quite comfortably. i've developed a close community of friends who share my environmental interests. the dating has even picked up although they've been short relationships. at least i'm not so devastated when these relationships end, and i'm learning to walk away with my self-esteem intact. i've even had the courage to end one or two myself instead of clinging on.

but it is time for me to finish the book. it's been collecting dust behind my desk for far too long. as i've been doing paid work for the past few years, the book has fallen by the wayside, and it is now time. please help me find the courage and commitment to see this through. i ask for Your help.

i give You my humble love,
Your daughter,

mare

CHAPTER 19

WHY?

JODY LEE MILES
AGE: 32

IT IS BECAUSE WE DON'T KNOW WHO WE ARE,
BECAUSE WE ARE UNAWARE THAT THE KINGDOM
OF HEAVEN IS WITHIN US, THAT WE BEHAVE
IN THE GENERALLY SILLY, THE OFTEN INSANE,
THE SOMETIMES CRIMINAL WAYS THAT ARE SO
CHARACTERISTICALLY HUMAN.

~ ALDOUS HUXLEY

From late 1997 to early 2001, I became more focused on doing environmental work and paying my bills, thinking that I could work on this book in my spare time. I found all sorts of other distractions instead. I realized that I was either going to commit to finishing it or give it up. I couldn't bear to think that all my work would go to naught, so I decided to end most of my projects, resigned myself to living very frugally, mostly off savings, and made a go of it.

There was one more interview that I had wanted to do before I felt all the interviews would be complete. For several years I had sought out someone in prison, but my efforts had all reached a deadend. I was repeatedly told that I needed to know someone personally in order to get permission to talk with them. Then in March of 2001, the

Baltimore Sun printed a cover article about death row inmates in the Maryland Correctional Adjustment Center in Baltimore. I did not even know that we had a death row in the city. I called the journalist to find out more.

There were several photos of an inmate named Jody Lee Miles accompanying the article. His case was also mentioned as a little-known murder case that was still under question as to whether it was self-defense. Other inmates were described, too ~ men who had murdered numerous women or other types of horrible crimes. Of all the inmates mentioned, it was Jody Lee Miles whom my instincts encouraged me to contact for a potential interview. When I mentioned this to the *Baltimore Sun* journalist, he concurred and remarked that, compared with the other death row inmates, Jody appeared to be a rather normal guy to sit and talk with.

So I sought out the address for the Maryland Correctional Adjustment Center and wrote Jody a letter introducing myself and my interest in interviewing him for the book. He responded immediately and agreed to do the interview in spite of the fact that all the other men on death row recommended that he not do it. It was clear that most inmates harbor a very large distrust of people in general, probably rightfully so. Thankfully, Jody was willing to take the risk.

Jody and I corresponded back and forth for five months, sharing stories about our childhoods and other parts of our lives. At the same time I explored how I could conduct an interview. I sent faxes to the commissioner's office and talked with the person in charge of public information. This was all taking place while Timothy McVeigh was awaiting his execution and then put to death in Indiana. I was concerned that the prison authorities in Maryland would react by limiting writers access to the death row inmates and that my chances to talk with Jody would be slim. Luckily, this was not the case, and they finally informed me of the policy that tape recorders were not allowed in the facility. But I could get on Jody's phone list, and he could call me collect from the one phone in his prison pod. I could tape the interview that way.

In order for Jody to call anyone, though, he had to put in a request that that person's number be added to his phone list. For two more months, his requests kept on disappearing into the abyss of prison bureaucracy. In the interim Jody wrote that he would prefer meeting me in person before the interview so he could have a better sense of who I was. This was understandable, so in early September, six months after I sent him the first letter, I summoned the courage to go to the Supermax facility to finally meet my "death row friend," as I started to refer to him. The facility is in a part of Baltimore that I would never want my car to break down in. After bracing myself for a disturbing glimpse into our penal system, I was turned away the first time I went. My name was not on Jody's visitor list although he had sent that request in a month before. So another set of phone calls was required to ensure that my name was actually put on his list, and the next week I tried again.

I went down to the Supermax facility five times in all. Amazingly, after the second visit I became quite comfortable breezing into the facility, showing my ID, going through the metal detectors, being escorted by armed guards through the multitude of corridors, listening for the very loud clang of thick metal doors behind me, sitting across from Jody in a narrow cinderblock booth with double-paned glass and hoping that the intercom system between the two sides of the booth would work. The only time I was thoroughly frightened was when I tried to make a quick visit to confirm our phone appointment. After Jody was escorted out of his side of the booth, I had to stand there behind the locked door and page the security station and wait for the guard to let me out. It seemed like eternity and, for the first time in my life, I felt imprisoned; a very unsettling thought occurred to me ~ I was at the mercy of a system that could easily choose to not let me out.

Everyone was so grim at the Supermax facility. They were clearly not used to seeing happy people, so I always went in with an upbeat sense of humor. I would smile warmly at the entryway guards and engage the guards in small talk and tease them about adding bells to their monstrous key rings to add more music to the symphony of metal hanging off their waists. You could always hear the clanking keys echo in the hall as the guards came down to the visitor booth door.

The Maryland Correctional Adjustment Center, or Supermax, holds the worst-of-the-worst inmates and the death row population of the state system. Jody explained that there were two pods of death row inmates and that each held about seven men. All the other men not on death row were murder convicts who had perpetrated other crimes after they were incarcerated. They had differing prison terms and were in solitary confinement twenty-three hours a day. It was certainly a violent lot, by all accounts.

I did not meet any other inmates, but I certainly got a glimpse of their visitors. They were all African American women, sometimes alone and sometimes with children. I wondered how many of these women and their children lived in the projects just several blocks up from the prison. The only other white woman I saw was a minister who made regular visits to an inmate who had originally written to over twenty ministers. She was the only one who responded to his letter and had been visiting him for three years.

The waiting room was a small, cramped space with two dirty couches bounded on one side by the security guard and metal detectors. The opposite wall was a glassed-in booth that seemed to be the security control center of the facility. There were usually several very tough-looking women guards there who would verify that our names were on the visitor list of the inmate we wished to visit. A TV with poor reception programmed to talk shows hung from the ceiling. Occasionally we would be subjected to a young mother verbally abusing her screaming child. Then the grimness of the prison settled into temporary misery for those of us forced to listen to dysfunctional family dynamics that were ensuring the creation of another generation of children destined for prison as adults.

Jody was a tall, thin, lanky man with clear eyes and a warm, coy smile ~ the quintessential "tall, dark and handsome" white man. Personally I found him charming, attractive and fun to talk with. He would crack jokes and tease me as we bantered back and forth. I believe he was quite the ladies' man before he was arrested. He had two wives and a girlfriend who were the mothers of his five children. The day before his arrest, he went out with five women ~ a feat few men could attest to.

During the half-hour visits with Jody, he told me more about his life and what it was like to be in prison. I learned about the realities of living where one never sees the light of day and guards are known to take a dislike to certain inmates and serve their own secretive punishments.

During these visits, he also explained his version of what happened that led up to his arrest for murder. He was managing an emu farm on the Eastern Shore of Maryland and was separated from his second wife at the time of his arrest. The facts were that a man was murdered during a loan shark pick-up on the outskirts of a neighborhood near where his wife lived. That night, according to him, he was at a bar seventy miles away, and there were eight people who witnessed him there.

The only evidence that the police had against Jody was that someone had taped the cell phone conversation he had had with his wife later that night. The way Jody described it, the murder was already news later in the evening in that small Eastern Shore town, and he had used his cell phone to warn his wife to stay away from that part of the town. They also discussed some other mundane issues such as his coming to fix a sunken hole in the backyard. An elderly man who eavesdropped on pornographic calls that he could pick up on cell phone frequencies happened upon Jody's phone conversation and recorded it and then turned it over to the police. Jody was arrested the next day.

Since I am not a lawyer and my intent was not to research his case, I simply listened to him talk about his case to better understand his background. By all accounts, he sounded like he was innocent and this was another example of a corrupt legal system. Then again, convicted people can create very believable but false stories about their innocence. I doubt I will ever know the truth.

By early October, we were finally certain that my number was on Jody's phone list, and we scheduled the interview. I had set it up that he would call me collect at a fax number at a nearby church where I knew the minister. I had heard horror stories of inmates calling numbers incessantly, and I wanted to avoid that kind of abuse. Jody called me right on time and we did the interview, seven months and many hurdles later.

✧

If I gave you God's phone number, what would you do with it?

Well, I'd definitely call and ask about a bazillion questions. Every question would be starting with "Why?" Why is this your plan? Why is this the path you set for me? Why did these things happen to me?

Something just occurred to me. If you were to call God, you'd have to get His number on your phone list! And then you'd have to call Him collect since that is the prison system. Let's say in your case, it's a 1-800 call. Don't worry, there are no charges. (Chuckling)

Oh, good, as long as we can get through, I'd have no problem then.

That's one of the qualifiers ~ everybody gets through. So when you say "Why?", you're talking about your situation and your case?

This and other situations in my life that I just don't understand. The first one would be the death of my twins. These were my first children, and they both died at birth after my first wife was in a car accident. One lived about an hour; the other one was only forty minutes.

Oh, my, what do you think God might say back to you in that case?

I don't know. I've asked just about every preacher I've seen or spoken to: "Why would this happen? Can you give me reasons?" They kept telling me stories about Job and testing faith. Those answers just didn't satisfy me.

Do you think anything would have satisfied you?

I don't believe so. I don't see any cause for their deaths. One of the reasons I left my last church was because the preacher could not give me any answers. It was a Christian evangelical church over on the Eastern Shore [of Maryland]. The preacher's name was Jimmy Holt* and he's on public television sometimes now. His church was called

---

*not his real name

Assembly of Spirit, and I was his youth leader for a number of years in the later '80s.

So you stopped going there?

Yes. It was not long after the death of my twins. I was having a lot of problems. I was trying to figure out why and I was asking him: "Why?" He couldn't give me a good enough reason. And it just didn't seem like he was the type of preacher figure I was looking for. My understanding was that Jimmy Holt had been kicked out of several other churches before for embezzlement. What gave me a bad impression of him was that he was living really well just a few years after he started the church in my town. He was buying his kids all kinds of vehicles, trucks, you name it. Then he got a house, and it wasn't any average house. He wanted to live on the golf course. Nobody else in his family worked.

Would you have any questions to God about this?

Well this man is supposed to be God's messenger. This is why I can't take a lot of things that these people say. If God could come to me directly and say, "Okay, this is why this is happening," maybe I could take it with more than just a grain of salt. But I don't have faith in these other people. If you have a lot of people that are preaching to you who you really can't take wholeheartedly, you have to decide what's truth and what's lies. You're probably going to take something wrong, anyway.

Okay, so you're saying your first question to God would have been why did your twins die? And you're not sure what God would say back to you?

No, I'm not sure. I just don't think it would satisfy me.

Even if God said it?

Even if God said it. I might think about it more. But my kids are the world to me. Just looking at them so innocent and for that to happen ~ it was just devastating to me.

Hmmm...So what other question would you want to ask then?

I'd probably go with my life itself. Like why did my relationships go the way they went? Why am I the way I am? My first marriage didn't work. That was doomed from the start, pretty much. But the pattern kept on. I married a second wife and we got separated.

I have tried to look for certain answers. In the back of a Bible I have, there is a listing of questions that you can look up. I've never found anything exactly like what I'm asking, but close. It still doesn't satisfy me.

So you have a Bible that you look at? What version do you have?

It's a student learner's type. I can't think of the name of it right now but it's something Student Bible. It's not like a regular Bible. It breaks it down as to what they're trying to say to you. A lady from New York heard about me and sent it to me in 1998. We're not in touch anymore though. [Chuckles] She wanted to marry me. Since I've been in here, she's actually one of four who wanted to marry me. Those are the people that really scare me.

Really? Would you want to ask God about these people?

I might ask God what motivates them to want to have me as their husband. They only know me from speaking to me while I am in prison. They only know me for the way that I relate to them. They don't know me. They know this Jody. They don't know Jody from five years ago. I think these women just see my personality. For instance, I like to make people laugh. At the same time, I listen. I want to hear their problems. I guess they're thinking that with all the problems I have, I'm still trying to listen to their problems.

The last one was a big shocker. She worked for a citizen's group that helps inmates. I had no idea she liked me. I don't know that I've led anybody on. It's just the way I am. I mean, I like to listen. There's still no reason for the marriage part of it. Why they would want that? Maybe it's just me. Maybe these women find some security in the way I treat them. I don't know. Maybe that's something they've never had, somebody that listens, someone they feel who's there for them.

Can someone actually marry somebody who's in prison?

Yes. But we're still in prison. It doesn't mean that we are released. They do a ceremony, and you get to kiss the bride, take pictures and then you're done. In certain prisons you can sleep together occasionally. This is super maximum, though. That's it. Then you go back to your cell area, and they continue to live in the outside world.

Okay. So your second big question was about relationships. What other big questions might you want to ask ~ here you've got God on the phone.

Why am I here? What is the purpose? They say God has a purpose for everything. What is Your purpose for this? I mean, I don't see it. There's nothing in the back of my Bible about being in prison.

And let's just say a person does commit the act of murder, they say God is supposed to be a forgiving God. Is this something that He is able to forgive a person for? Because if you ask for forgiveness before you die and He truly forgives you, then why are you still receiving punishment of death?

Right, because if God's forgiven you, then every human being should be able to forgive you, too. Yet how would God communicate that to all the people on Earth who are involved in the legal system? "Oh, we got a fax from God today. He said He's forgiven Jody Lee Miles. Well, we better let him go because God sent us a fax." That would be highly bizarre. (Chuckling)

Well, one guy here made that point.

I see a lot of people come to prison and become religious. It's called "jailhouse religion." You don't see too many people in here without a Bible. They want to be forgiven. But chances are if you freed these people today, the first thing they're going to do is go out and sin. The Bible would be the last thing on their mind. They'll go out and go back to their old lifestyles of drugs, drinking, whatever. You won't see them praying out there like they do in here. Maybe they're thinking there's some sort of freedom or a way to get out of this if they just pray hard enough.

What do you think about that?

It hasn't worked for me yet. I can say that. And I pray a lot. I've never stopped praying since the early 1980s. I pray every day. I may not do it like those who bow their heads before they eat so people can see them. I'm not in this for show 'n' tell. I'm walking around day and night praying and asking God, "Why is this happening to me?" Or, "God, take this away. This is too much of a burden for me." I do this all day long, a hundred and fifty times a day.

Somebody may be getting on my nerves too much that day. I'll say, "God, why am I putting up with this? Why is he doing this to me?"

Do you ever get any insights that help you from all this praying that you do?

It only helps in a sense because I feel like I'm getting something off my chest. I'm speaking to somebody. Yeah, it relieves some of the pressure. I don't know what that makes me as far as being religious. I pretty much believe, but I'm not like the Holy Roller-type person.

Before you were arrested, did you pray to God as much?

Not as much. Believe it or not, there wasn't as much stress out there as there is in here. There're so many different mentalities and things you are forced to deal with here. We all live pretty much in a box. Out there, there wasn't quite as much I felt that I had to pray about. But I still did it but not quite as often as I have to now.

Jody, can you tell me who God is to you? When you pray, do you have any kind of image in your mind?

Well, the one you see of Jesus on all the pictures everywhere. I look at God and Jesus as one and the same. I imagine that He is the image of a perfect, sin-free individual. If I ask myself the question, what would God do? ~ I think I'm probably going in the right direction.

Although I don't know if I'm really imagining anything while I pray. I'm really just praying. That's it.

I wonder if you might have any questions to God about dying and what happens after you die.

I do wonder what they are talking about in church when they say life after death or eternal life. I always heard it in the prayers. Obviously after you die you don't feel, you don't touch, you don't sense. All your senses are gone. So literally, can you break down life after death? I have no clue what they meant, but that's my question. But I don't know what the answer from God would be, either.

I think about what happens after people die, and what puzzles me is whether ghosts exist. I've been watching the show Crossing Over with John Edward, and it makes me question that maybe there is something there. Maybe there's a whole party going on over on the other side.

What did you think of death before you started watching Crossing Over?

You're just dead. That's it. End of story. But my mom would tell all these stories about ghosts. She's convinced that we lived in haunted houses. She would talk about all these military boots she used to see in the hall, but when she'd come back to get them, they would disappear. Once she put a coffee cup on the table in front of her husband, and it moved to the far side of the table. She actually talked to the ghost and told it to leave the coffee cup alone. I would take her out to dinner, and she'd even tell the waitresses some of these stories, and I'd have to make a sign to them to ignore my mother ~ you know, that sign that someone is a bit crazy.

So would you have a question to God about this?

All that time I thought my mother was just wacko. But then this Crossing Over show is on the TV and you start to think, well, maybe...Is there any truth to the possibility that there may be ghosts?

What do you think God might say back to you?

Well, I don't know. But if they do exist, how do I become one? I think that the best option would be to become a ghost when you're dead. Otherwise I don't know where you go. I could still amuse people. That's all I'm shooting for. I think people would forget about you otherwise.

You already feel like you're dead here in prison. The people closest to you, or you thought were close to you, totally ignore you. They don't write you. They don't come to see you. You can call and most people here do. But out of respect, I don't because if I call my family, it's always collect, and it's about fifty dollars every time. So I try not to call anybody.

So what I hear you saying is that you already feel like you're kind of dead being where you are right now. If you were to die with the death penalty, it might not be that different because people already don't care and have forgotten about you.

Not that I want to die from the death penalty, because I don't want to, but misery is just a common thing here. And if you passed away, there would be no more misery. Sometimes you think it might be better to die. If you're stuck here in the prison system for a long period of time, it's a slow degrading death, anyway.

People do not pay that much attention to you anymore. I don't blame them. But at the same time I think about all these people I've helped while I was out there. Now I can't even get a simple birthday card, not even a "How ya doing?"

So you would look forward to being a ghost?

Exactly. Because it would be more amusing. And people

would never forget me. I'm not saying that people don't give me a thought now and then. But these people never try to contact me.

Jody, do you think everyone who gets the death penalty goes to the same place, assuming that there is a place that we all go to after we die?

I really don't know. I'm hoping my twins are in a better place. I really don't know where they are, but I've got this image of Heaven with clouds and the Pearly Gates, and I hope they're in a good place like that. There was a man who died by the death penalty in Maryland a couple of years ago, and he was Islamic, so I'm not sure if he went to the same place as my twins. If there was only one place, I do think everyone goes there, if God is a forgiving God as they say. Islamic people have a different opinion of who is what or who does what, though.

That gets a bit interesting, doesn't it?

Everybody interprets the Bible in different fashions, too. So that's a little confusing to me. But another thing that always used to make me mad is how some people can claim that they are Christian by going to church on Sundays. Yet the other six days, they're cussing, screaming, kicking, drinking, doing drugs. But they say they're Christian because they go to church that one day a week. These people have tried to sit there and judge me when I didn't go to church for a while. They'd say to me: "You're not even going to church." And I'd just tell them: "Yeah, but I'm not doing all that crazy shit you're doing all week long, either."

So the question is, who's the real Christian?

I've never made any claims that I don't sin. I know I do. But these people are supposed to be religious, holier-than-thou folks. But they don't want you to see what they're doing. I catch 'em doing different things. If God can forgive these people for the sins they do all week long, then wouldn't He forgive everything that you ask for forgiveness for.

Tell me, is there any minister or priest who talks to you there?

We have a guy called Father Chuck. I have no clue what religion he is. He came in to see me the first day I came in. He didn't even tell me who he was. He just started saying, "I just came in to see if there's anything you want to talk about." I had just arrived, and I was really angry. My first question to him was, "Who are you and why are you taking up my time? I don't know you and you don't know me, but yet you're in here. I just got sentenced to this. I'm not a happy person. Why are you talking to me?" He just sat there and said, "I'm Father Chuck."

He also looked like a mess. I'm thinking that's not what I perceive a preacher to be. Looks can be deceiving ~ I understand that. But his hair was all every kind of way. His shirt was wide open. I went back to my cell and looked on the news to see if there was a hurricane outside. I thought there must have been something going through out there. He just looked so bad. I didn't understand that.

I mean, you have to understand my mentality at the time. I had just arrived. I had been sentenced to death for a crime I still maintain I'm innocent of, but yet this priest comes in taking up my time. I don't know him. And I'm not in the happiest mood.

Yeah, you were pretty upset.

Right after I was sentenced and before I came to the Supermax in Baltimore, I was put in solitary confinement. People said that I took it really well and they couldn't understand that. But what can I do? My actions weren't going to change anything, so I just had to believe that there was a purpose. I just didn't know what it was yet.

It sounds like you're still grappling with what that purpose is. Do you have any inkling as to what that might be?

Not really. I just don't understand what the purpose is. I know that I listen to people, especially other inmates. I'm the one they go to. I feel like I've helped them in a lot of ways. And I'm good at keeping the peace. I tell them I'm here to listen if you need somebody to talk to. I'm not being egotistical, but I'm probably the most levelheaded person in here. I think they like it also because I don't judge. I tell everybody we're not here to judge nobody. Who are we to judge? That's my insight as to what I think is going on.

So do you think you've changed at all since you've been in there?

Oh, I think I have changed in a lot of ways. I wasn't always as understanding. My temper's pretty much gone. There were things that used to make me really mad, but I wasn't a violent person ever. I've never committed a violent act. If I got mad, my thing was, I wouldn't talk about it right then. I would just say, "Leave me alone" and I would walk. I would leave my vehicle and walk. I walked fourteen miles one time. I was pretty angry.

The thing was, I was actually hoping for a ride. I started out walking mad, and I was in my cowboy boots, and they were very uncomfortable to keep walking in after a few miles. But all these people kept going by me. I was going to a meeting hall fourteen miles away. I got almost a block from the hall, and then these people pulled over and said, "Do you need a ride?" And at that point, that made me really mad. I said, "Man, where was you thirteen miles back? I don't need a ride! I'm going right there!"

You got angry with the people who offered you a ride? (Laughing)

Because where were they thirteen miles ago? This is what I was thinking. I look at it now and laugh.

So you don't have this kind of anger anymore. Do you get angry about anything right now?

I used to get mad at the attorneys because I feel that they are the reason I'm here. They didn't argue. They didn't help me. They didn't do anything. Maybe they thought they were doing what was best. I don't know. I've just become more accepting. Whatever happens, I'm prepared for it either way. I just let it just roll off my shoulders ~ that's fine.

In what other ways do you think you've changed?

I really think I'm pretty much the same person, except I do take people's feelings into consideration a little bit more than I did during my dating days. With the women who proposed to me here in prison, I've tried to be sensitive and told them all the same thing. I told them that I don't think it would be wise to consider marriage at this point in my life. I have nothing to offer, really. This is not the way for a marriage to start off. The ones who didn't take it well or became more demanding, I just said, "Look, I think it's best we remain friends, but let's not talk as much. Let's not write as much."

There're other ways that I've changed positively. I'd

definitely say my eyes are open more now. I don't take as many things for granted. I don't make snap judgments about people like I used to. Now I look for the better in them. I'm more open to people's feelings or emotions and try to understand them, not judge them.

I've tried to get the inmates here to look in the same direction and not take the anger they have out on other people. I've become more like a mediator in here. Whether I'm qualified or not, I have no clue, but if it gets it done, great. I don't always have the answer.

I think I'm a much better person than I was then. I'm not saying I was an awful person then. I've just changed.

You know we were talking about trying to figure out the purpose of your being in there...

Maybe that was the answer to my question. Maybe God wanted me to be a better person or to be more open to people's feelings and not take things for granted. Maybe He wanted me to see what I really did have at certain points in my life and that I may have very well screwed up on my own, but I didn't see it at the time.

It sounds like you've done a lot of reflecting about different times in your life since you've been in there.

Well, yeah, I certainly have a lot of time to do that. You look at a certain situation and you think about the what-ifs. Like the other night, I was watching TV, and there was a man talking about doing time travel. Automatically my mind switched to all those things I would have changed if I could go back. There were just so many situations I would have done differently. At one point I had the world, and now that's gone.

So perhaps you would do it differently now. Jody, this is

a tough question for me to ask, but they gave you the death penalty. Do you grapple every day with the fact that you may actually still get it?

Well, I'm prepared in a sense. Realistically, I'm not afraid of dying. I'm more afraid of how people will look at me after I'm dead. My biggest concern is how my kids will handle this and the fact that I was not able to prove myself. They'll have to say to their friends, "My father died on death row." My oldest son, who is fifteen, has already gone through a lot. People have said to him, "Your dad's a killer." "He's on death row." That put a lot on him.

The dying part is not what concerns me. I don't want to die, but I'm not afraid of it. I've been thinking about this for years, and this is my reality. It's my kids and what they'll go through. But I'm still confident I'll walk one of these days. I just don't know when.

Do you talk to your children very often?

Very seldom. Their mothers go through stages when they'll talk to me or not. There are three women I had children with. Two I was married to and the third was a girlfriend who was supposed to be on the pill. I have five children. There wasn't supposed to be as many as five. I love my kids and all that. But my second wife got pregnant just as we were separating. I didn't know she was pregnant. And then this other woman, she said that she couldn't get pregnant. And then they both came back to me around the same time and said they were pregnant.

I said, "Well, you're pregnant, she's pregnant." I didn't know who to be with. And they both were very jealous people. They both didn't like each other. It was a dilemma. Trying to go to doctors' appointments with both of them and everything. At least I made sure that it was not the same doctor.

Jody, you have an interesting life. (Chuckling) Hmmm...It really sounds like the hardest thing is how your children will handle it ~ if this death penalty goes through.

See, my point is that I just want to be able to prove my innocence, and then I can concentrate on being a father they can look up to. I want to be that kind of person because I never had that kind of father in my life.

I never even knew who my father was. I've never met the man. My mother told me who he was, but if you do the math, it's feasibly impossible for him to be my father. My uncles told me it couldn't be him.

I know you told me that your childhood was pretty tough.

Yeah, it was a very abusive childhood. My mother was married ten times, so I had a number of stepfathers. Most of my siblings are from different fathers. I got married twice. I'm not that far up there. But it apparently runs in the family. Only one of my direct siblings has been married once. All the rest have had more than one spouse.

So, we still have God on the phone here, and it's your choice when you want to hang up. Although I guess there at the prison they decide when you hang up. The operator comes in and tells you ~ what was that? ~ "You have one more minute."

They tell you when you have two, and then it comes down to one minute, thirty seconds and then that's it.

That's it, cutoff time. Well, let me assure you that if you ever call God up outside of prison, there's no limit. There's no angelic voice that comes in and says, "Oh, honey, you have thirty seconds left." (Laughing)

There was quite a bit on my mind. If I had God on the phone and my time ran up, I'd be upset. I'd be like, damn, it took thirty-two years to get You on the line, and now You hang up, thirty seconds left. Isn't this something?

That would happen only in prison because they restrict the calling time. So how would you end this conversation with God?

Well, first I would make sure that I got my time in. And I may pass the number onto some other inmates here but only after I finished my whole time period with God. Let me get my time in. It's taken me all my life to get You on the phone. I'm going to be selfish right now.

Right. But suppose I said to you that you could call up God anytime. This is not your one and only opportunity.

Well, while I had a train of thought, I'd want to get all of it out. And then, by all means, whoever wanted to use it would be free to use it. Although I would pass the phone over if I saw that another inmate needed to speak to Him far more urgently than I did in that moment. But this is my quality time with God.

After I hung up the phone with Jody, I knew I needed to be still for a while to fully absorb the interview. It was still light outside, so I walked to the park near my house. I reached an open meadow and sat on the warm grass. Once there, my feelings could truly surface. For the first time since I had started the book ~ six years ago ~ I felt awash in humility. Who was I to have these conversations? Who was I to ask these people to talk about God with me? As I sat there on the ground, I knew that it was a deep honor to be able to do these interviews.

Finally recording that interview with Jody was an accomplishment. I have to admit that I approached talking with a death row inmate with some preconceptions. I thought Jody would want to only focus on his fears of dying and his tough existence in the prison. I thought he would be far more self-absorbed. But this was a man who was more concerned about his children than anything else. His first question to God was about his twins and why they had to die. I was surprised.

Jody is the only person I've spoken with who thought that even God's answer might not satisfy him. In my experience, most people acknowledge the omniscience of God and His word's being the ultimate truth. Yet here is a man who would still question God's answer. After I questioned Jody about God, his responses led me to believe that he perceived God as more of a perfect person and not the Creator. I guess if you imagine God as more a person than the Ultimate Being, it's easy to think you would question that person's answer. This was still a novel concept to me.

The issue of God's forgiveness is a big one. What if God does forgive a heinous criminal while they are still alive? If God's slate is wiped clean, then why couldn't our imperfect human system of serving justice be wiped clean also? Jody raised some good points here.

But it does seem that our set of systems here on Earth is very separate from the universe's. I think sometimes we fool ourselves into thinking that our system is aligned with God's. But from my limited exposure to some of the inefficiencies ~ not to mention possible corruption ~ in the prison system, it would be difficult to think that all the work there is God's work.

There are so many jokes about St. Peter sitting at the gates of Heaven as a bouncer, filtering out those who don't belong in the Godly celestial realms. I'm not sure about large golden gates with a booth that St. Peter sits in at the side. The implication with that is that the rest of Heaven is surrounded by barbed wire electric fencing so a soul can't sneak in beyond the gates. A scary thought and certainly not the concept of Heaven that I was taught while still a young Catholic girl.

Surely there must be some sort of system in place in the universe to process or even punish souls who have done dark deeds. Then perhaps God forgives them once they have learned their lessons. Perhaps forgiveness is arrived at only once a person or a soul has made amends and shifted him or herself.

I think about forgiveness in my life. Each time I have really tried to forgive, it is only because I have tried hard to understand why that person would hurt me. I've tried to look at what pains are in her life that made her want to lash out at me, her childhood, her husband, her depression etc. Last year one friend I was just developing a friendship with lashed out at me so strongly that I was in shock for several days. She was unemployed, and I had been trying to help her, and she greatly resented my style of "helping." Her coarse words over the phone slapped me so hard that I reeled with anger and deep hurt afterwards. It took me weeks and talking with other mutual friends for me to understand why she might have reacted in such a way. And gradually I came to forgive her.

What I've come to learn is that the pain that people have caused me is something I can choose to use, either to open my heart or further calcify it against them. This is a process for me that I still fight sometimes. It is hard to completely let go of the pain and consequent distrust. I can only try to chip away at it. For me to forgive someone for murder, that is a whole different realm. And I think only God would be able to know all the facts (other than the murderer himself) to even begin to forgive or serve appropriate punishment.

Jody questioned how his preacher on the Eastern Shore could afford the cars and new house. This left him with a lifelong distrust of those who claim to speak for God. I can't blame him. There are so many preachers who do claim that their work is the work of God and yet we hear later about how they've been caught with their hands in the till or with their secretary in the back room.

Jody really seemed like a nice guy. Yet I'm reminded that neighbors of Jeffrey Dahmer said the same thing about him. The only thing that made me question Jody's goodness was when he talked about his anger. How could you get angry at a driver who's offering you a ride just because that same driver wasn't there thirteen miles back? Jody also told me during one of our prison visits about how he got seven speeding tickets in one day because his speedometer was broken. I had never heard of this rate of tickets. As he was telling me about it, he still seemed angry it. After the second ticket, he knew something was wrong. He just could not understand that it was his responsibility to monitor his speed and get his speedometer fixed. I teased him about this but still walked away with a funny feeling that there was a disconnect here.

The most challenging aspect of the interview with Jody was not knowing how truthful he was with me. From the way he talked, he appeared to be a reformed person ~ if indeed he was the person who shot the other man on that fateful night. If he did not do it, then this was another example of how our justice system has gone wrong. Jody claimed that the reason he was convicted and given the death penalty was that it was an election year, and some politician made it his goal "to serve justice." I'll never know.

One part of the case that Jody shared with me was how the prosecutors brought in all the women he was dating at the time of his arrest. It was a large number. According to Jody, all these women really liked him and had nothing wrong to say about him ~ until they learned that they were only one of a stable of women he was involved with simultaneously. One question that I really wanted to ask him but just couldn't because it was too value-laden on my part was, if God is a woman, perhaps this is why he was now serving time!

CHAPTER 20

REAL SUCCESS

ABDULLAH
AGE: 45

A SIMPLE PRAYER

LORD, MAKE ME AN INSTRUMENT OF YOUR PEACE.
WHERE THERE IS HATRED...LET ME SOW LOVE.
WHERE THERE IS INJURY...PARDON.
WHERE THERE IS DOUBT...FAITH.
WHERE THERE IS DESPAIR...HOPE.
WHERE THERE IS DARKNESS, LIGHT.
WHERE THERE IS SADNESS...JOY.

O DIVINE MASTER, GRANT THAT I MAY
NOT SO MUCH SEEK
TO BE CONSOLED...AS TO CONSOLE,
TO BE UNDERSTOOD...AS TO UNDERSTAND,
TO BE LOVED...AS TO LOVE,

FOR

IT IS IN GIVING...THAT WE RECEIVE,
IT IS IN PARDONING, THAT WE ARE PARDONED,
IT IS IN DYING...THAT WE ARE BORN TO ETERNAL LIFE.

~ ST. FRANCIS

In early September of 2001, I was working intensively on completing this book. I had conducted what I thought were all of my interviews and was almost finished with the writing phase.

Then September 11th happened. Like many, I was quite shaken and horrified at the terrorist attacks. But I knew these events must be symptomatic of some deep cultural and spiritual dysfunctions. Why would people from another country and a vastly different culture so hate us that they would attack us in such a way? As the days passed, I began to make more sense of the whole situation. More than anything, I knew that there was a gap in this book ~ I did not have any Islamic perspective on the question.

Given the chaos that we were all swirling in, it was important to find someone Moslem from the Middle East to interview as opposed to an American-born Moslem. Since the terrorist attacks were believed to be the work of Moslems from the Middle East, specifically Osama bin Laden and his terrorist network, al Qaeda, a Middle Easterner might shed some cultural light on the whole situation in addition to responding to my questions about God's number.

A friend of mine who is a member of a Sufi group in Philadelphia named the Bawa Muhaiyaddeen Fellowship♦ told me he knew someone from Afghanistan. Sufism is considered the mystical tradition within the Islamic faith. This Afghani man was the mu'adhdhin, or the man who gives the call to prayer to invite the Fellowship community in for the five daily prayers. He suggested that I call the Fellowship to find out more. So I did and was able to contact Abdullah, a forty-five-year-old man originally from Kabul, Afghanistan, who was a resident of the community. Abdullah and I spoke over the phone briefly, and he agreed to let me interview him a week later in Philadelphia.

♦For more information about the Bawa Muhaiyaddeen Fellowship and published works by Bawa Muhaiyaddeen, go to www.bmf.org.

As I drove north the following week, I reflected on the bombing that had just started in Afghanistan and the anthrax letters circulating in the mail. I wondered whether people living in Philly were washing their hands after they opened their mail the way we were in the Maryland-D.C. area. We were all living in a high state of alert, especially on the East Coast where all the terrorist activities were taking place.

And here I was ~ meeting an Afghani man who lived in a Sufi community. It crossed my mind that perhaps this man could be part of the Osama bin Laden network of contacts, but I quickly dropped the thought for it did not seem possible that a terrorist would be living in a spiritual community. I don't imagine terrorists being very spiritual, in contrast with what Osama bin Laden had said in his videotaped speeches.

Abdullah had given me very clear directions to the Fellowship building. It was in an upper-middle-class neighborhood on the outskirts of Philadelphia. Yet once I got to the correct street, I drove by the building three times before I realized that it was the right one. I was expecting to see a large golden dome on a mosque-looking structure. Instead, it was a very large formal home with huge white pillars on an expansive lot, looking very similar to the other prestigious homes nearby. The only distinguishing characteristic was that the front yard was a paved parking area instead of a lawn. I discovered as I was leaving at the end of the afternoon that a smallish mosque with a gold dome had been built onto the back of the large home, very discreetly hidden from the street.

After I parked my car and knocked on the front door, a fair-skinned, slender woman in her late forties wearing a shapeless, light blue dress and shawl welcomed me in. She instructed me to take off my shoes just inside. This I did, immediately noting that I had worn the most colorful socks I own ~ a pair of bright, striped socks that I proceeded to pad around the building in for the rest of the afternoon.

Another woman went to summon Abdullah while I was introduced to several others, all in their later forties or fifties wearing scarves over their heads. The room we were in must have been the original living room, hallway and dining room of the expansive house but was now a large meeting room with colorful Arabic paintings and rows of collapsible wooden seats that looked like used high school auditorium seats. The room could seat close to one hundred fifty people. At the front of the room was a raised dais with an oversized chair on it ~ I assumed for a teacher to sit in.

After a few minutes, Abdullah appeared. A handsome, agile-looking man of medium height, he was dressed in a simple cotton shirt and work pants. I could see immediately that he was a forthright, confident, yet gentle man. He invited me to follow him to an empty common room to talk. After we sat down, I noted that Abdullah's coloring was an almond tone, and he wore a uniquely shaped tuft of a beard on his chin. On his head he wore a small felt cap that covered all of his hair. He explained later that Moslems always cover their heads, and his wife made his hats especially for him. What struck me the most about Abdullah were his brown eyes. They were so bright and clear and warm. It was obvious that this was not only an intelligent man but a good, kind man.

The interview started off with Abdullah, telling me about the Bawa Muhaiyaddeen Fellowship. Bawa Muhaiyaddeen was a Sri Lankan Sufi sage who had many followers while he was living in Sri Lanka and was invited to move to Philadelphia in the early '70s. Bawa, as he was called, was considered one of the more evolved Sufi masters to live in the United States. He died in 1986. The Fellowship has continued to publish his teachings and expand its community of people interested in his mystic Sufi wisdom. At present about fifteen people live in the Fellowship house while hundreds more attend prayer there. There are also satellite communities associated with the Fellowship in several other countries and across the United States.

Abdullah also explained how his life travels had taken him from Kabul, Afghanistan, to live in a Sufi community in Philadelphia. He had always been a seeker. He had started traveling to see the world in the mid-'70s and was going to return to Afghanistan, but the Russians had invaded the nation in 1979. So he, along with several brothers, became political refugees in the United States. The Church World Services found a host for them in Philadelphia, and hence they settled there.

Even as a young boy, Abdullah wanted to know God. Therefore, while he attended a trade school and found a job as a librarian at a major hospital in Philadelphia, he continued to search for God and truth. One of his colleagues, knowing his hunger for a teacher, told him about Bawa Muhaiyaddeen. In time, Abdullah moved into the Fellowship to commit himself to his spiritual path.

Abdullah's responsibilities at the community were to maintain the buildings. He had a background in auto and building repair, so he was kept busy between the five daily prayers as a jack-of-all-trades for the community. He lived with his wife in a small apartment there.

Because Abdullah's experiences had been so powerful, we first talked about his spiritual path as a prelude to the question.

✦

Abdullah, can you tell me about finding your teacher?

I was searching so much. When I first arrived in the United States, I went to a few Sufi meetings here in Philadelphia and in New York, but I hadn't found my teacher. I knew that I was looking for a Sufi master. You need to find somebody who has traveled the path and has gone to the very end so he can guide you. You can't just find any amateur. The amateurs with a few fancy words are out there. No, I was seeking somebody who knows the hidden path.

You specifically wanted the Sufi path and not just an Islamic community? Why?

To know God, you have to go to somebody who really knows God intimately, who has firsthand experience of God. Not somebody who has read about Him. If you go to the mosques or religious places, they can only tell you what they have read in the books, and that's not what I was asking. I wanted somebody who has firsthand experience of God. Not only that, but one who has emerged and disappeared in that divine love. I was seeking one who himself has lost his ego in that divine love. Because the goal of Sufi is the divine love. I am sure of that.

What do you mean by "lose your ego"?

My teacher, Bawa Muhaiyaddeen, taught us that we need to die before we die. This is very similar to Jesus saying, "Unless you are born again, you will not enter the Kingdom of God." What Bawa meant is that we have to die to our personality, to all of our negative thoughts and emotions and qualities. Die to it means actually transforming it, transforming our evil qualities into good qualities.

Another way to say it is that we need to identify with our divine self instead of our lower nature or ego self. And it can be done. It is not always fun and can be painful at times because we hold onto that lower nature. But all we have to do is let go. Release it.

But we don't know where we're going to go when we do

let go.

That's true, and I know. Because I have had experiences of fear. What will happen to me ~ that ego part, me? That is the ego saying: "What will happen to me?" I examined that me, and I discovered that me doesn't really exist. It's just in my imagination. I imagined myself to be separate from God and therefore that me, which is a little ghost of just thoughts, is what is scared of annihilation. When you examine deeply, you find out that me doesn't really exist. What really exists is that consciousness of the soul that is the life of this body that is within every human being.

In truth, how could it be scary losing your ego when you lose such a little trickle, just a little teeny, tiny ego which is causing so much trouble to then disappear into that infinite ocean of love? How can it be scary? It is a most beautiful place and is infinitely welcoming. It is joy.

I used to go out and pretend to be homeless as a way to let go of my ego. This was joy for me. I was holding a good job at the time, but I wanted to shrink my ego. I would get dressed up in tattered clothing and spend two to three days on the street just several blocks down from the hospital library where I worked.

Every time I would beg, I would beg with complete humility. My beard was long and I had long hair, and people would come up to me and say that I looked just like Jesus. I wasn't trying to look like Jesus.

I experienced so much love doing that. When love is there, then people can see something different. There's beauty there. We just love them because they're our brothers and sisters because that is truthfully what we all are. We have to become totally insignificant in our sights to see this. But I wouldn't recommend that everybody start begging to experience this.

That is so powerful. So, anyway, can you tell me a little more about finding the Fellowship?

My friend had suggested that I come and meet Bawa Muhaiyaddeen, and when I did, I was certain that he was a true sage. This was a true human being ~ not just a Muslim. I knew that this was somebody who had found God, and he was in direct contact with God every moment. You could see his holiness as he was walking down the stairs. I could see and feel that he had almost no weight. He floated down the steps. Somehow God gives you grace to see sometimes, and I could see this.

When Bawa started teaching that day, all he said absolutely resonated with what was in my own heart. I could not believe that such a man really existed on this planet and right in Philadelphia. I couldn't stop crying.

I feel like crying hearing you say that. (He was so heartfelt in this part of the interview that it almost brought me to tears.)

Nonstop. Tears were flowing down my cheeks through to the end of his teaching. You see, a year before, after several years of traveling all over the world and then moving to Philadelphia, something happened to me one day in 1982. Suddenly this voice from deep within said, "Who are you? From where have you come?" Not from what country ~ but who was I spiritually? "What are you doing here? What are you supposed to be doing here? What is your mission on this planet? Where will you go next?" The questions came out of nowhere. But it opened a gate to my heart, to myself.

These questions took me into the depths of my soul. I had never heard about meditation before, and I didn't know how to go into silence before that day. But after that I would just spontaneously go into the very center of my being and meditate. It was beyond the realm of intellect. I became aware of the subtleties of human life and many,

many realities.

What do you mean by the subtleties of human life?

Who we are. Being a human being is not what it appears to be. We are so much more than the physical. There's so much more to who we are.

After that initial experience I felt like the love of God was gushing forth into my heart, and I was drowning in it almost twenty-four hours a day. I could feel His presence every single moment of every single day. And if I did not feel His presence for one moment, I would cry in utter desperation, "What have I done? What can I do?"

I was still in vo-tech school, and my teachers there asked me what happened because I used to be so happy. I told them I didn't know. All I knew was that I had lived for myself for twenty-five years. And now I needed to live for God.

With that awakening of the heart, I also started perceiving the suffering of mankind. I cried endlessly while communicating and convening with God. "Oh, God, You have to help my brothers and sisters. Not just Muslims or Christians or Jews or Afghan ~ no, all mankind."

That went on for a long, long time. I was still living with my brothers, and one of them told me that I couldn't live with them like this. I was always crying in my bedroom. I had to go to the roof of the house to cry. And then I started walking in the woods crying.

It went on and on, but then I began seeing visions of my spiritual teacher and that he was waiting for me. I had no idea who he was. At the time, I was seeing many visions of how I was doing on the path and things in my life in the future. Eventually I met my friend who told me that I should come and see Bawa Muhaiyaddeen. When I saw Bawa, I knew that he was the teacher that I saw in my visions.

I did not move right into the Fellowship at the time. I chose to wander more and do odd jobs, but eventually God led me back to the Fellowship, and my teacher invited me to live there in community with him and others. I finally felt like I had arrived. I realized later that Bawa knew all along that I was to move in.

I have since come to know that my duty was to be here with the master. I believe that my teacher arranged it for me to come here. He was with me everywhere I went. The masters, they have infinite powers. Their realms are too incomprehensible. These teachers can see absolutely everything. When anyone came to Bawa's presence, it was as if a scroll would come down in front of him and tell him everything from the day that person was born.

Mystics see all this in order to help you see what section of your heart, what quality needs to be replaced with what other qualities, and what you should do to overcome that. They see everything about you in detail. They see the future. They see with the light of God. They can see the beginning and the end of time ~ everything.

And now you're married?

Bawa chose my wife. We do not have any children. It was she who wanted to marry me for a couple of years. But I didn't know because I only wanted God, nothing else. I wasn't thinking about marriage. But he thought it would be good for my spiritual path to marry her. He asked me a couple of times, "When will you get married?" I said, "Bawa, lonely come, lonely go." But eventually I understood. I consider marriage as just the workshop now. It is the best place where you can erase your selfishness.

Okay. Can you tell me a little bit about your responsibilities here at the Fellowship?

I take care of the mosque and Fellowship buildings. I open and close the doors most of the time. I also clean the buildings and take care of things that have been broken.

Another duty I have is to be the Mu'adhdhin or the one who summons the faithful to their knees. You pronounce it "mwa-then." The Mu'adhdhin sings in Arabic to invite those outside to come inside and pray. The prayer that is sung is the following:

God is great. God is great. God is great. God is Great. There is no God but Allah. There is no God or deity but Allah. I testify that Muhammad is his messenger. I testify that Muhammad is his messenger. Come to prayer. Come to prayer and blessing. Come to success. Come to success. God is great and the greatest. God is the greatest. There is no God or there is no deity but Allah, the one God.

What is meant by "success" in that prayer?

Real success comes from God, not from our worldly achievements. The true mission of our life is to realize God and to realize our selves. That is real and enduring success. Success that is received through the hands of man is temporary success. A successful banker has only temporary success. If a fanatic comes along and takes a plane into the World Trade Center, it is most unfortunate, and all of what that banker has accomplished vanishes in a second. What they have lost is not real success. It only appears to be.

Very interesting point. Perhaps now is a good transition for the question: If I gave you God's phone number, what would you do with it?

That is fine. We have to pause for a moment because I have to go inside.

237

[Long pause ~ He then speaks as though he is in an altered state ~ his expression more somber and voice in a much deeper tone.]

First and foremost, I would have to know God in order to invite people to God. My deepest desire and intention is to summon all mankind to God. But I have to know what kind of God we are summoning people to. I wish to know God intimately and absolutely. Not imagine that I know God ~ no ~ to experience Him in absolute fullness.

So if you were to give me God's number, I would call in that moment and say to God, "You know what I want. Here is my life and here is my heart. Here is my existence. I give it back to you in completeness so that I may know You absolutely."

(Pause) Do you already have God's phone number? I have the sense that you developed a strong connection in 1982.

Now and then. [He nods his wrist to convey sometimes.] I have always loved God. Even as a little boy, I had incredible love for God.

I was never a religious person. Even now, I do not consider myself to be religious. But I do consider myself godly.

What does religious mean to you?

To be religious is for novices in the training period. It's not your eternal identification. Our eternal identification is that we are all lovers of God, servants of God. One aspect of your personality is involved in being religious when you practice or fulfill God's commandments. But I don't worship religion.

To me, religion is a path upon which we walk to draw closer to God. But the idea is not to stop on the path and adorn and worship it, saying, "Oh, this is the best path and yours is the worst path and you will go to Hell." That's not the point. It's just a path to walk upon to reach God. But many people worship the path itself. Many people get stuck in certain places on this path and they are not continuing all the way to being God-loving.

I don't know how many people really know that they are walking on this path toward God. I think most people practice their faith for several reasons. They hope to gain Paradise. Or they think that by worshiping God they will get a lot of good things in this life. Or they pray, "Oh, God, spare me from getting hurt, getting sick. Spare my family." And they also pray, "Please destroy my enemies. Rain your stone punishment on the neighbor." That is the kind of religion that a lot of people are involved in.

Abdullah, how did you develop this way of thinking about religion? Was this something you saw people doing in Afghanistan?

I see it all over the world. I see most people acting like this. I don't see people being God-loving. I mean, I cannot judge because it's an impossible thing. God knows best, but if there were that many godly people we wouldn't have come to such a mess.

I'm talking about what's happening in the world now. Especially after September 11th. All the terrorist activities. All the Muslims trying to kill the Americans. They don't even know that they've killed about four hundred and fifty to seven hundred Muslims just in the attacks on September 11th. I don't know who really did it, but if it is indeed Osama bin Laden then he is the first person who would be burned in Seventh Hell. That is the worst, deepest, bottomless pit of Hell.

God has said in the Holy Koran that anyone who deliberately kills a believer of Muslim, if a Muslim kills a

Muslim, his punishment is hellfire beyond a shadow of a doubt. And God's wrath is upon him and God has cursed him and prepared the severest punishment for him.

But Osama bin Laden is hoping they are going to be blessed by God and elevated.

Osama bin Laden imagines that he's on God's side. When I see him on the videotape and I hear his words ~ I see the anger, revenge and hatred in his heart, and this is not what God is. This is the work of the Devil. This is what I see when I see him. He thinks he is doing God's work, but this is not God's work.

He is interpreting God's message to serve himself, to serve his intentions, his purpose, his hatred for America, his hatred for Israel. Through hatred, you will not gain closeness to God. Through hatred, we develop a good relationship with the Devil.

Hatred and God, there are two completely different things. God is love. In the beginning of each chapter in the Holy Koran, it starts with "I begin with the name of God, most compassionate, most merciful." In every verse, in every chapter.

Would you have any questions to God about how it is that someone like Osama bin Laden could so misinterpret His teachings?

I would ask God, "Bring the criminals to justice." Whoever they are. If this is the work of Osama bin Laden, then he needs to be brought to justice, too. God knows who they are.

And spare the innocent people from being killed here or in Afghanistan, anywhere in the world. For God loves it most when we make a good intercession that is full of compassion and love on behalf of humanity for the sake of unity.

Abdullah, do you pray in the Sufi tradition?

We do, according to Islamic tradition based on the
Commandments of God. It is said in the Holy Koran that a
Muslim should pray five times a day. We try to stand in the
presence of God and feel His presence and do our prayers
during these times. They are written prayers from the Holy
Koran. At the end of our prayers, we can supplicate
whatever is in our heart. These are personal prayers.

What I would say in my personal prayers is, "Oh, God,
please unite humanity. Show them the way to true unity
and happiness, peace and love. And show them the way to
self-realization above all because we have identified
ourselves with our cages." Our cage is our body.

I may pray also that these criminals be brought to
justice, but I wouldn't pray that all the time. But I do make
a special prayer every time asking God for peace,
happiness and safety for all human beings.

**I notice, Abdullah, that when you start talking about
Osama bin Laden, your whole body language seems
to take an angry stance.**

I'm not angry. But I do not appreciate hearing about
people who cause the indiscriminate massacre of innocent
lives in the name of Islam. Islam is such a beautiful religion.
It's absolute purity and beauty, bliss and joy. The holy
prophet, our prophet Mohammed, peace be upon him, says
a Muslim is he from whose hand and tongue all lives are
safe. Islam is, "Love thy neighbor as thyself." You cannot
hurt anyone. This is the message of Islam.

Of course in that sense, I am upset, or even you could
say I am angry, yes, because I don't like this kind of
injustice being done to Islam. This kind of terrorist activity

being done in the name of Islam. It has nothing to do with Islam. It's pure demonic actions.

These are not human beings who have committed these acts, not even to mention they are Muslims. They have nothing to do with Islam. They are not even human beings. I believe the Devil is very active right now. He has been active on this planet from time everlasting. But he is active more so now than ever before.

Why do you say that the Devil is more at work now than he ever has been on the planet?

Look at what is happening around the planet now. What is the Devil's joy? What makes the Devil happy? To create fear, terror in the hearts of man. To create anger and all this anguish. To make this uncertainty, to make people forget God.

The best defense against this kind of situation is that we embody all of God's goodness and qualities. This I know. All I ask is for peace and unity among mankind. I would even ask God to help bin Laden or anybody who is committing this kind of terrorist activity to become a good man. I wouldn't pinpoint him because I don't know whether they have the absolute proof that he led the September 11th attacks. But I would ask God to help whoever it was to die to their evil qualities and their selfish motives and make them a symbol of love and peace and unity. What loss is there for anyone when bad people become good?

We each can do our best. We can shield or ward off this kind of evil by becoming good ourselves. We need to dispel all the selfishness, all the evil qualities within ourselves to become a channel of peace, a channel of love. As the prayer from St. Francis says, "God, make me an instrument of your peace, where there is hatred, let me sow love... " It is a beautiful prayer. You see, I respect and learn from all faiths.

[His watch beeps.]

I have ten minutes until afternoon prayer.

Oh, we have only ten minutes. I do have one big question left for you: Who is God for you? Do you have an image?

God does not have an image. He does not have form. God is formless. He is the infinite divine love. In the Holy Koran, God says that He is closer to a human being than his jugular vein. He is with you wherever you may be. He is our very own life. Nothing exists without God. Even the chair there has God in it, and that is what gives it its awareness. I don't know how much awareness, but it has some.

When I was little I could feel God all around, but I never pictured Him as being an image. But I knew God was love. But when you are little, you think that you are separate from God. You think God and me. But I don't think that I am separate from God now. No one is separate from God.

It says in the Holy Koran that when He fashioned the body of Man out of clay, He breathed His soul into that form. That is the reality of Man. How much closer can you be to God? He breathed His essence into us, which we identify as our soul. Our soul is our life. Our soul is our essence.

The holy prophet, peace be upon him, Mohammed, said, "He who knows himself, knows his Lord." What he meant by that is that He who truly knows himself knows himself as one with God, not as such and such an Afghani. That is not our self. That is our false identity that we identify with our body and our personality. When people say, "I was born in America, I was raised in Philadelphia...," these are just little fake stories. The real story is we existed before this form. And we will exist after this form. So, then, who am I? That is the question.

[Pause]

I know I must go to pray now, but I will continue the conversation there. One can never say goodbye to God, thank God for that. I will ask God there: "Please provide Your guidance, Your light, and Your love and Your forgiveness for all humanity. Please guide humanity onto the path of self-realization and pure presence."

So you don't see yourself hanging up the phone?

I don't know about hanging up the phone. I try to always be with God. Sometimes I'm on the Internet, so I guess I do hang up sometimes. Or when I go to sleep or read the news.

But I do know that I would give the number to everyone, all mankind. God is closer to us than our very own life. He is our very own life. And I want everyone to know that. Absolutely.

✧

(Prayers were about to start in the mosque, and I wanted to stay for them, so Abdullah found another woman in the Fellowship to guide me, and then rushed off. This was the same woman, Cater Beebe, who greeted me at the door earlier in the afternoon. Cater Beebe quickly led me to the only women's section of the Fellowship into an odd bathroom with a wall of low spigots where she modeled how I was to ablut or wash myself appropriately to go to prayer. Then she wrapped my head in a long scarf, and I quickly followed her upstairs to the ceremonial part of the mosque, a large, open room with a small semi-circular chamber in the front and a round skylight framed with Arabic writing beneath the actual exterior dome.

It was midday on a Wednesday so there were few people there, mostly those who lived in the Fellowship. The women were cordoned off in a back section behind the men. Cater Beebe motioned for me to stand between her and another woman and to follow her movements through the whole prayer service. Much of it involved kneeling and bowing down, touching your forehead to the ground and then squatting back up while responding to prayer. Thank God it was carpeted. My bright, striped socks sandwiched between the other women's thick, white socks made me giggle inside. Clearly I hadn't gotten the Sufi dress code down before I came, I thought.

The prayers were over quickly, and Cater Beebe led me downstairs to the kitchen area in the Fellowship. Abdullah greeted me there with a big smile. Just moments before, I had seen him through the screen that separated the men from the women in the mosque, checking to be sure that I had made it into prayer. He offered me some tea, and we started talking more. I realized that I still had further questions for him, so he honored me with several more minutes of interview.)

✧

Abdullah, in the Islamic or Sufi tradition is there such a thing as a spiritual warrior? I know there is talk of the Jihad, the Holy War these days...

When the prophet Mohammed, peace be upon him, conquered Mecca, his birthplace, he conquered everyone with love. He conquered everyone's heart. There was some fighting, but for the first ten years he did not fight. The Muslims came to him and pleaded that they be able to fight. They had lost their homes to the infidels when they were forced out of Mecca. Some had lost their wives and children.

So finally Mohammed, peace be upon him, asked God to show them the way. And God's command came, "Yes, go, fight. But fight in the way of God." There were about a hundred conditions. A holy warrior should not hurt children or women, not kill livestock, not cut down the trees. It made it so difficult to fight, not like nowadays.

People say Holy War these days, but they're full of Hell themselves, full of evil qualities, and then they try to fight what they call a Holy War. Holy War means we ourselves have to be holy to fight the Holy War. But people don't understand this. They learn a few books and then they say, "Now I'm going for Holy War." Holy War means you're fighting for something that is holy. If we are not in the state of being a holy person ourselves, how can we fight a Holy War?

But there is another meaning to Jihad or Holy War. After the Muslims took Mecca back, Mohammed, peace be upon him, said we have come from a lesser Jihad or Holy War and we are entering a Great Holy War. The people asked him: "Oh, prophet of God, so many people have died in the past, and so many atrocities have been committed. How can you say that this has been lesser?" He responded that the war they had just won was minor compared to the battle against our own egos and evil qualities and thoughts and desires.

So the real Jihad is this internal battle against evil inside ourselves. One must fight for truth only, not for the sake of hostility, hatred, anger, revenge or anything else. It is to help the truth overcome falsehoods. It is to release people from their bondage to their evil intentions and qualities and evil ways of life and to bring them to goodness. That does not require guns. Certainly there are times when there is a need for self-defense, but this is not Holy War.

Before we can take arms, before we can even attempt to go on the outside to convert others, there has to be a Holy War inside ~ a Holy War in the name of truth against the evil that is really the enemy of every human being.

This Holy War that Osama bin Laden is calling for is not at all what has been taught?

No. The Holy War is to conquer evil within us. It's really an individual battle. When we conquer the evil or the ego that is reigning the terror right now in the world, then we find that we have reached a place of love and unity with all life. We will never hurt anyone. We will never take up arms to kill somebody because we have merged with the compassionate God. We have merged with the love of God. There is no place for hostility. There is no place for killing another life. There's only freedom from ignorance with the weapon of wisdom and love and compassion. God says, in the Holy Koran, "Invite them to the path of your Lord with wisdom and good qualities."

Are there people who are Islamic missionaries who go into other countries?

Yes, but they just learn a few books, memorize a few passages from the Holy Koran and sayings of the Holy Prophet and they think they are ready. They are not ready. You have to learn how to be a true warrior before you can even invite people how to fight against their own evil qualities. When we are full of evil, how can we invite others to conquer evil in themselves?

It's not enough just to call people, or to invite them to come to embrace Islam, when we have not really become Muslim. Muslim is not just by the name. A true Muslim is he who has completely surrendered his will to the will of God. And he is carrying out only God's will from that moment on. Only then can he invite people in the way of God.

How many true Muslims are there, then?

I hope there would be about ten. That would be a good number. Maybe increase it to one hundred. I don't know. Bawa said he can't find a really true Muslim, one in so many millions, because they would be in a state of Divine love in the state of the Omnipresence.

So one out of every million, that would be very good. And that is very, very hard because nobody wants to really kill their own egos. It's painful. You just want to learn a few books and teach your ego Islam. That's a very bad choice. And it's very dangerous because then fanaticism creeps in very quickly.

Fanaticism is what creates the thinking: "I'm right and they're wrong." It is the ego and self-righteousness that is at the root of that. Whether they are Christians, Jews or Muslims, any who think: "I am better than my neighbor" ~ that signifies the Devil has planted himself deep within that person. Because you never consider yourself better than another person. We have such little knowledge about what's really in the other person's heart.

When we see that God has created all men in his image, how could one be better than the other? You just have to look at everyone with the eye of equality. Men and women. The spirit of God is no less in a woman than it is in a man.

Abdullah, help me understand this. Why do the men stand further up front than the women during prayer?

Prayer is like battle rows. The meharab, where the leader of the prayer stands, means the battlefield. We go there to fight our evil qualities and thoughts. I would say both men and women have determination. Women have more love, but men have more physical strength. There are certain times such as during menstruation when women are not allowed to pray. Of course, there's no war. We're not really fighting anybody. We're fighting our own evil qualities to try to conquer them and to change them to the ways of God. It requires a lot of strength. Women do serve and they are of great importance to Islam and to every other religion and to the whole world.

What is your perception of the Taliban's treatment of women?

It is very wrong what the Taliban have been doing to women. This is very un-Islamic. Not letting them out of the house or work and beating them if they show an ankle or their eyes. This is a cultural thing and has nothing to do with Islam.

And the covering of women from top to bottom, that is not Islamic. God has commanded the believers in the Holy Koran that all women need to cover their heads with scarves in prayers, and to draw their veil over their bosoms so that they will not entice men to lust. This is to protect them. Men wear hats all the time, too, just as with the Jews, because the top of the head is the crown of God.

But Mohammed, peace be upon him, does not say to put the bag over your head. That is not God's commandment. With the Taliban, women can't even show their eyes. Probably you have seen them on TV. They put a bag over themselves that completely covers them from top to bottom with only a tiny screen in front of their eyes to see through. This is not Islamic. This is the Taliban.

Tell me, what does the Islamic faith teach about dying?

In the Islamic faith, when you die and you are in the grave, you go back to the realm of the soul. Two angels come to inquire about the good and bad you have done. There's a place of waiting somewhat like purgatory. If we have done good things, then God will open the Gates of Paradise, and the nourishments and the fruits and joy and pleasures of Paradise will be open to us. But if our evil outweighs our good, then we will reap the harvest of our evil actions, which means we will be tasting all the horrors we have committed and we will be experiencing them in the grave of the mystical.

Does your faith talk about reincarnation at all?

That is something I do not have authority to speak about. In Islam there isn't such a thing. The mystics may speak about it, but that's a different story. The mystics look at it from a different perspective. They may look at it as every time we come here, we can grasp only so much of our true nature and the reality of God and the experiences we have on this plane. So, for instance, the blind person cannot say that he had the fullest experience of life. So he may incarnate again for a more full experience.

Our teacher did speak a little about this, but generally Sufis refrain from speaking about it. We don't want to open up that can of worms.

Okay, I won't ask any more about it. I do have one last question: do you consider yourself a mystic?

I hope...when my ego and my personality are totally dissolved and there's nothing but that Divine essence, then I would consider myself a mystic. Right now, I'm somebody who's aspiring to be a mystic.

Do you have any final thoughts?

It is time, Mare. The truth will spread throughout this Earth very soon. It will happen when we surrender. When we recognize what I think I am is really a dream, but what I really am is the spirit that always dwells with God. That is surrender. Surrender means that we surrender to love. We surrender to goodness. I believe it has to happen through His love and His grace.

Right now ignorance is reigning this world. It doesn't matter what we call ourselves, whether we call ourselves Christians or Jews or Muslims ~ that's really irrelevant. What is relevant is that we are not using our love and wisdom and our goodness to overcome things. Most everyone has given in to their ignorance in allowing their minds to run the shop.

We all need to do what we can in the name of goodness. That's all. I'm not even concerned about the religion itself. What I'm concerned about is about good and bad. If we become totally good, if there's no evil inside us, then none of these worries would happen in the world. That's it. To know to surrender.

✧

I was deeply, deeply moved by this interview with Abdullah. How ironic that it took the events on September 11th to compel me to seek out such a God-loving individual. It was doubly ironic that, in spite of all the negative perceptions of the Islamic faith within the United States after the terrorist activities, it was an Islamic person who was one of the most spiritually awake individuals I found in all my searchings.

Abdullah is truly a mystic although he would not claim that. The man is in touch with God in ways that I can only dream of. Or perhaps I can aspire to.

Interviewing Abdullah was an emotional experience for me. When we first started talking, he was somewhat reserved, but the more I questioned him and listened, the more he spoke from the core of his being. I almost did start crying at one point as he spoke about his spiritual awakening at age twenty-five. At a certain point about halfway through the interview, I think we both recognized that we were brother and sister on the spiritual path, although our paths have been quite different. I had certainly never been drawn to join a Sufi community, and he was not participating in Native American sweats. Yet we both were seeking ways to become more God-loving, and we recognized that in each other.

Abdullah saw me out at the end of the afternoon, and as we said goodbye he touched his hand to his heart. I felt the same way. We had made a heart connection that day. It was not a romantic heart connection but a spiritual connection as if we were saying to the other: "I see you, and you are a beautiful person inside. You are me. We are both one on this path of being with God."

The timing of the interview with Abdullah was profound. I had been going through a stage in my writing where I knew that it was my fears that were holding me back from finishing the whole manuscript. I had just interviewed the man on death row and was very humbled by that experience. But I was still tussling with my fears to try to shrink them down so they could fit in a small side cupboard and not be the two-ton gorilla pack blocking my path and feeding my procrastination with big handfuls of fancy chocolates. I knew that my fears were intimately tied with my ego. Lo and behold, I find a person to interview who speaks to this very process as part of the path to connect with our higher self and God. It was only right.

There were many things that Abdullah brought up that gave me more clarity. After he mentioned the prayer of St. Francis, I made a point to revisit that prayer when I returned home. It is a hauntingly beautiful song on one of my tapes and also in a frame on a bookshelf. The last line of the prayer had never made sense to me until Abdullah's interview. "...It is in dying...that we are born to eternal life." Perhaps St. Francis was speaking to the need for us to "Die before we die." Just as Bawa taught it. We need to kill our ego in order to really overcome our feelings of separateness from the Divine, in order to really recognize that we are part of God.

I did some further research into the Christian concept of being reborn. From what I could gather, this is largely the same concept. However, being Reborn in the Christian tradition seems to be framed around the whole concept of being a sinner, which I am very uncomfortable with. I can accept, and aspire actually, to having my ego die (and this will not be an easy death, for sure!) and feeling myself become one with God. But if I need to get there from the place of beating myself up for being a sinner, then I cannot do it, since I do not believe that I was born with "original sin." My whole being balks at taking that path.

Another point that Abdullah made that was very illuminating was about religion. He made the distinction between being religious and godly. As he put it, most people get stuck in religion and don't realize that it is a path to continue along to become God-loving. For some reason, while religion does play an important role in helping people start on their path, it does not necessarily encourage people to be God-loving as their ultimate goal. When Abdullah talked about the various things that people primarily pray for ~ comfort, health, Paradise/Heaven and punishing their enemies ~ he encouraged me to think. Perhaps he is right. And, if so, how did we ever lose sight of what our true purpose is?

If people did really understand that our goal is to merge with God, not necessarily financial security and comfort, would the whole world be made up of children, mystics and saints? Surely we would not complain! Everyone would recognize their healing and be far along the path of being healed to be one with God.

I really did not want to stop talking with Abdullah, for there is so much that this man is in touch with that I seek. I knew this. I seriously considered how he and I could continue to talk and whether his Sufi path was the right one for me. Conceivably I could drive up to Philadelphia on a regular basis to participate in their prayers. I could purchase books written by Bawa Muhaiyaddeen and may still do this.

I reflected on this for several days after the interview, but my instincts kept on saying "no." I realized that, much as the Sufi path offers great wisdom, I could not fully join it. I was not comfortable with the suppression of the feminine essence that I experienced. I believe very strongly in the spiritual presence of Earth Mother and the strength of the feminine as it is expressed as intuition, compassion and fertility in spiritual principles. The little bit of time that I spent at the Sufi mosque in prayer that day left me with the impression that that particular community, perhaps all Islamic communities, are afraid of the feminine. They certainly want to cover it up.

Of course the Taliban took it to an extreme, and Abdullah made the point that that was a cultural phenomenon. But it is easy to draw the link between the suppression of the feminine with the abuse of the Earth. I couldn't understand why women are not allowed to pray in their community if they are menstruating. Is this not part of the natural cycles of nature that proclaim that a woman is able to give life? Wouldn't this instead be something to celebrate with God?

Women seek to be as close to God as men do. Sometimes I wonder if there are not more women seeking to be closer to God than men. In all the spirituality workshops that I've taken, there have been far more women participants than men. This makes me believe that women are innately more drawn to develop their spiritual sides.

It is still difficult for me to understand why the men need to stand in front of the women at this mosque. It strikes me that this Sufi community reflects some of the values of all patriarchal religions, embedded in the patriarchal societies that frame those religions. These religions deny the concept of an Earth Mother spirituality ~ which our planet is so in need of. Our dominant modern-day society would not be needlessly destroying the environment if there were a greater recognition of the spirituality inherent in the Earth itself.

So I come back to my own path. I continue to pick and choose and learn from those I speak with about God. Abdullah reinforced what this path is for me ~ to be God-loving. I would only add to his words that it is important for me to be Earth-loving also. It is my belief that in practicing both, honoring God the Creator and Earth Mother from whose womb my body developed, that I come closer to my true spiritual self walking this planet I call home.

CHAPTER 21

ANYBODY CAN TALK TO GOD

JASMINE HISHA
AGE: 44

I LOVE TO THINK OF NATURE AS AN UNLIMITED
BROADCASTING SYSTEM THROUGH WHICH GOD SPEAKS
TO US EVERY HOUR IF WE WILL ONLY TUNE HIM IN.

~ GEORGE WASHINGTON CARVER

I have saved this last interview for the end of the book even though the interview was conducted in 1997. When I met Jasmine Hisha, she offered me answers to almost all the questions I had about God and the Universe in ways that I never could imagine. Meeting her was a significant turning point in my life, and she actually became my spiritual teacher.

Jasmine is a Cherokee teacher of shamans. A shaman also goes by the term "medicine person" and is someone who works with the spiritual realms to promote healing. I first heard about her through a friend who had been seeing her for some back problems. I shrugged off the thought of seeing her as a client at the time because I had no idea what she did.

Several months after I returned from the Omega Institute in 1996, I was feeling quite emotionally lost. I had gone back on antidepressants and was seeing a therapist, but my dark mood continued for months. My heart was in so much pain, I remember it aching on a daily basis, and it was all that I could do to get out of bed in the morning. Bed was such a place of security. I did not have to deal with anyone, accomplish anything or take any risks if I just stayed there. I was not seeing any light in the midst of my despair and could not pinpoint any particular reason for my emotional malaise, fearing that this was going to be my existence until I died. My friend mentioned that Jasmine was leading a sweat one Saturday and perhaps I might be interested in meeting her.

So I drove out into the countryside of Baltimore County to see if I might finally meet this Cherokee shaman. I could not stay for the whole sweat since I was busy later, but I wanted to spend a little bit of time with her to see if I could get a sense of who she was.

I arrived at the farm where the sweat was being held, and it was not hard to find the sweat lodge and fire circle on the edge of a large piece of woods below the farmhouse. It was a women's sweat; there were about nine women there, including Jasmine, all hanging around the fire in lawn chairs. My friend got up to greet me, and she introduced me to her healer and the others.

Jasmine had the broad cheekbones that I had seen in other indigenous women, but her skin was lighter than I expected. She was slightly overweight with a light almond complexion and large gaps between her teeth. Her hair fell long and black and straight to below her waist. When she saw me, she got up and gave me a strong warm hug. I immediately got a deep impression of Earth Mother energy. It was clear that Jasmine had a strong character and big heart. We did not talk very long, but I knew when I left that I had never met anyone like her before.

Another month passed, and my depression sank deeper. Gardening season was over, and it was all I could do to raise myself to make it to my temp work on time. I remembered Jasmine again and, desperate for any help, called her. She astounded me. She definitely remembered me and proceeded to tell me all about the things that had been going on in my life for the past six months and how a healer I had seen at Omega had triggered this particularly debilitating spell of depression.

She explained that the other healer had not healed me but only shifted me. Just as shifting a broken arm can be excruciating, this healer had shifted my psychic body, and hence I was in severe emotional agony. It all made complete sense to me. Yet I had told her nothing and there was no way that my friend could have given her all that detail, for I had not told my friend that much about the other healer. It was amazing. Jasmine already knew all of these things. The most powerful thing she told me was: "I can help you." For the first time in my life, I felt like I had found a healer who could truly help me lift from the clouds of despair that had haunted me since childhood. After talking with her for about forty-five minutes, I scheduled a session, and we ended the conversation.

The following week I drove down to Jasmine's house in a nondescript neighborhood in the suburbs of Washington, D.C. Her husband was in the military, and they had been transferred there several years before. Jasmine met me at the door and welcomed me into her den where she had candles lit on a small table laid out with a circle of various stones and animal carvings. I remember thinking: "Ah, so this is how a shamanic healer works."

Starting with that first session, I began to visit Jasmine on a monthly basis for healing work and teaching. I had no idea how she did what she did, but I knew that I felt better and stronger each time. When I asked her to explain to me how she healed, she would laugh. She told me that it was the energy of the Creator and Earth Mother passing through her that allowed her to do her work.

One day Jasmine pulled out a piece of paper and drew

her family tree to show me how many shamans/healers were in her family from both sides. Clearly it was in her genes to be able to put her hands on people's bodies and have them walk away without that back pain or knee ache. Over time I realized that she had the ability to scan people's bodies to see what physical ailments they had, as if she had x-ray vision. She could see tumors, where vertebrae were out of alignment and a multitude of other physical issues. She also could perceive each person's spiritual body.

During one session, she told me that she was going to work on my heart to heal it. She said that this would help me get over the lifelong pain that had shut down my heart. I stood in front of her, and she placed her left hand on the center of my chest and sang a sweet little song to me. The song was actually to distract me, she explained later. Later that evening I can remember feeling as though I had been drugged. She had sent a tremendous amount of energy through me. And gradually I sensed that my ability to be more compassionate and sensitive was opening up. It was incredible the abilities that she had, yet she used them with the deepest humility.

I went off the antidepressants shortly after that first session in 1997 and have never gone back on them. Beyond the healings, I loved her philosophy on Earth Mother and the Creator. Plus she was very funny, loved to tell ribald jokes and had the most wonderful deep laugh. Just being in the presence of her laughter was a healing experience!

Several months after I started seeing her, I approached her about my book and a possible interview. Here was a woman who had such a different perspective on spirituality and God. I knew that I had to interview her. She was very open and thought it was "cute" that she could be part of my book. We did the interview in her house one afternoon.

✦

If I gave you God's phone number, what would you do with it?

If you tried to give me God's phone number, I have to tell you that I already have it. And I use it. I use it every day. It helps build up a resistance to bullshit. [Laughing]

I talk to God every day about whatever is on my mind. It might be my husband, my daughter, my dog, my cat, my friends, whatever is on my mind that day. And He talks back to me. That's what makes it fun. Of course He mostly laughs. He laughs because I'm only a human being and I'm funny to Him. He finds me humorous because sometimes I think I'm important. "I talk to God...Aren't I special!" God laughs at me then. But anybody can talk to God. You just got to do it.

Have you always talked to God?

I have talked to God every day of my life since I first learned words. My grandmother taught me how to do this. I call it connecting. I connect when I wake up and before I go to bed. I can do it outside or inside, standing, sitting, even when I'm pissing. It makes no difference where I am.

In the morning I go out and call: "Hey Ho ~ thank you that I'm sucking air another day. By the way, I'm really annoyed about such-and-such." Or, "Thank you for helping me out with such-and-such. I really appreciate it." And I get a low giggle, like a baritone giggle almost. Another time I might say: "You know, I'm really angry about something, and I'd really appreciate if you'd do something about it." And again, I'll get this low giggle. And He'll say back to me, "I already knew."

God's voice is nice and low and gentle. He might tell me, "Daughter, don't we know better by now?" Or, "Daughter,

261

were you or were you not raised to be a warrior? You know what to do."

My conversations with the Creator aren't any different from my conversations with a friend. I'll ask a question, and He'll respond, "Well, look at the answer." I usually am clearer then, but sometimes I feel stupid that I could not see the answer myself.

There are times I want to yell at the Creator. I want something and I'm not getting it. And I'll blame God just like my child blames me. He really laughs then and there's a whole chorus that joins in: "Check her out. Look at her stomp her foot! She thinks somebody gives a rat's ass! Ain't she cute!" [Laughing]

Then I take a deep breath and I go, "Okay, you're trying to tell me I'm not going to hit the Lotto, right? This is what you're trying to tell me, I'm not going to hit the Lotto, right? I'm not going to get $10 million." [Laughs again] "But I want it!"

Earth Mother speaks with me also. She's chatty. Her voice is very different from God's. It's very melodious. She gives me good wisdom whenever I ask for it. I might say to her: "I gotta do such-and-such today, Mom. What do you think I oughta do?" And then she'll give me a great suggestion. It's usually something that I had not thought about in a long time, and I'll tell her that and thank her.

So you talk to God and Earth Mother all day long?

Yes, my conversations really don't end. I talk to God and to Earth Mother throughout the day. I just chitter-chatter during the day. "What about this ~ oh, okay, I see that." "Well, what should I do about ~ oh, okay." And on and on.

The Creator and Earth Mother's messages are clear to me because I've developed a relationship with them. People in mainstream society are not taught that they can actually have a relationship with God. They think they've got to go to someone else to intercede for them. That is not the truth. That has never been the truth. We all can communicate directly. That is the truth.

I don't just talk to the Creator and Earth Mother. I talk to all the trees. I talk to the brook. I talk with the swan family in the spring. They talk back to me, too. They were the first ones to tell me that there are bobcats in the woods beyond the houses. I went looking and found that was true. I also talk with the geese. They share what it was like up north with the weather changing with global warming. And I answer their questions because they have questions, too. I like talking with the Canada geese because they see so much from year to year because of the amount of land they fly over. We have really great conversations. But anyone can learn to do this.

We all can develop the sensitivity to hear the voice or the voices. It's called expanding one's mind. And people in this society are just not encouraged to do so. They're encouraged to be robots ~ to do everything like everybody else.

There is a simple recipe for talking to God. It's always best that when you talk to God, call It by whatever name you're comfortable with calling It. It could be God, Universal Creator, Allah, Brahman ~ whatever. Then claim a relationship: you're Its daughter or you're Its son. It's important to claim a relationship. And give it the one thing in the universe that does not automatically belong to the Creative Force: your love.

It will take time to hear a response. You need to develop your relationship. It's like meeting somebody new. First you feel each other out. But after you continue to go to lunch with each other every day for a year, you are going to be quite chummy and telling each other all kinds of things. It takes a while to create a relationship even with God.

Every day before meeting with any of my clients, I will

ask the Creator and Earth Mother to help me. When I do my healing work, it's not me doing the healing. It's Father-Mother's energy moving through me. This is what allows me to do my work. My connection with them is deep.

There was a time when people were more connected to the Creator and Earth Mother. The positive and negative energies on the planet were balanced then. Literally everything on this planet has an energy, positive or negative. These energies used to be balanced, but they are not any longer, and that's the problem. It got thrown off when we began to lose our sense of spirit and our connection. We started getting greedy and hoarding. To get it back into balance, we need to let go of these darker sides. We need to start connecting with the spirit of the Creator and live in less fear. And people can learn to do this directly. They don't need to be in organized religions to do it.

It sounds like you are rather judgmental of organized religion.

I have promised my true parents, the Creative Force of the universe, that I would not become aligned with any of man's religions, that I would stay free of the dogma. The spirit is changing these days. There isn't going to be any more room for Buddhism or Christianity, no more foo-foo shit. People are tired of being hungry, of being victimized, of being shit on. Buddhism in its pure form is beautiful. Christianity in its pure form is beautiful. It's all the bullshit people have put into it over the couple of thousand years they've both been in existence that has taken all the power and beauty and simplicity out of it. These religions teach people to be passive. They teach their people to be sheep. "Your good shepherd will take care of you." This has not helped a lot of people.

Most Buddhist practices are teaching a meditation

practice that encourage people to empty their minds. Why in the hell do you want to empty your mind? What is the point? They have made it totally complicated. But if they taught the simple process of just being quiet, it would be different. If you just become quiet and still, then all sorts of solutions will pop into your head. The Creator can then communicate with you. But if you empty your mind, how are you supposed to get an answer to something? What's the point in sitting there being all still if you're not looking for answers? Otherwise, you'd be better served getting up off your ass and doing something. This is very old knowledge.

When people empty their minds, they are shutting the Creator's wisdom out. There's enough mindlessness in the world ~ we don't need to encourage this concept. If people want to be mindless, vacuum the floor. You don't need to think, just be mindless, vacuum the floor...And you're empty, you're mindless.

Are you saying that your native traditions have no form of meditation?

Tiyoweh is our Native word for real meditation. It means being still, having inner stillness. But most teach meditation as far more complicated than that. They say you've got to have an altar and sit there and contemplate your navel or chant OM. Sound has great power to it, but not when you're sitting there being mindless with it. Then it's just a noise. You might as well listen to the refrigerator tick. People can learn instead to still their minds to listen to the Creator speak and find their power within.

Take some of the Christian dogma ~ they would have us believe that homosexuality is wrong. But that's their personal opinion. The universe doesn't give a shit. The Universe loves it when people love...period. What are you pumping into the universe? If it is love, that's great.

Morals by the universe are very different from morals according to the Christian perspective. That is why, as far as morals go, Native peoples are considered very tolerant. We don't consider ourselves tolerant, just civilized. We have no problem with homosexuality. When two people love each other ~ fine. And when the Christians pulled fidelity on us, we didn't understand. We believed if you loved a man and he loved you, you could bond and have kids. But it wasn't necessarily a lifelong commitment. Why should it be? People change and love other people.

There's a right way to do things and a wrong way to do things. Take the New Age movement. I've already allowed myself to be talked into playing around with some of this New Age stuff, and this has really angered me. Much of this is like following false gods. The amount of ignorance, the massive "uneducatedness" of it all is very sad. Channeling is one small aspect of it. Calling up the spirits is another. New Agers like to do that shit. It's so stupid. It's like giving a two-year-old matches. What they're doing is calling up negative spirits. These people think it's wonderful when good things happen at first. But these spirits are like the pedophile who first offers the candy and then has other motives. The spirits they call up do not have good intentions. It's very dangerous.

Jasmine, how would you describe yourself?

I'm a wonderful, wicked, wild woman. [Deep laugh] And I help people clean up their shit. I am able to communicate with the lightning to stop it or bring it on. I exorcise people, houses. This spring I'll be healing a farm so that life can spring up again. The ground there has been killed by all the chemicals. I heal cats, dogs, birds, trees. I'm working on the oak tree at the bottom of the yard. I can do all kinds of things, and I will do more.

But getting back to calling God ~ the Creative Force

finds us adorable actually. The Creative Force loves us. And It's actually thrilled when we turn to It and give It our love so that It is able to move in our lives.

There are different personas in this Universal Force: the Creator, the Creatress-Earth Mother. That is an is. That's not because of my culture or my mindset or my perceptions or my opinions say it is. Earth Mother appears to many people. Some call her the Virgin Mary. She doesn't care. As long as you call on Her with love and are willing to be healed by Her and turn around and heal others, She will hear you and answer you. Yeah, I talk with Her every day. And She hears me.

✧

As I suspected, this interview with Jasmine was a blast. She is a fascinating woman. I came to realize that what she shared with me in this interview was true. She really did talk with the Creator and could hear His voice along with Earth Mother's. She was born with this ability as many shamans are, I believe.

From when I was a child, I sensed that nature was where God could be felt the most. It was certainly where I found peace when my parents were arguing. The graceful arching branches of trees created a cathedral that always beckoned me to be still and listen. Trees seem to embody a wisdom so much more ancient than ours. So perhaps it was only right that I find a teacher who would help me go deeper and find peace with a path I had embarked on long before I met her.

My real shifting and healing took place when I found Jasmine. She embodied a sense of Earth Mother that I had long yearned for subconsciously. She helped me learn more about healing and spiritual ways than any other teacher I had met. Since I met her, I have shifted so much. I no longer wake each morning with a deep sense of dread about my day. Instead, I wake with a feeling of excitement and anticipation of what adventures lie ahead for me on that day. Occasionally I'll lapse into some down moods, but I quickly bounce back again. More than anything, I have learned to cry and experience joy as I never could before. It is as though she has helped me clean out my entire emotional body to be more balanced. I'm still in process, though. I know I'm not a finished "piece" by any means.

Jasmine also taught me how to connect with the Creator and Earth Mother as she described Them, and I have now been doing this for almost five years. And gradually I have come to hear answers. I don't hear the distinctive voices that she hears, but I do occasionally receive guidance when I connect that helps me resolve issues that I'm grappling with.

When Jasmine talked about meditation and questioned why people would want to be mindless like that, it prompted me to remember a friend who was heavily involved in Vipassana Meditation, a form of Buddhist meditation. This friend would participate in silent meditation retreats for as long as forty days. One time he had just returned from one and, according to him, the main event of the retreat was how there had been a glob of jelly on the dining hall table one day. It appeared he had obsessed about this jelly for several days, if not longer. Perhaps he had had moments of divine bliss, too, but it seemed that he spent more of his time focusing on some spilled jam. I really was not sure what he had gotten out of that experience. Jasmine's point about learning how to be still to listen for answers as opposed to meditating makes great sense to me.

It was also interesting to hear her talk about how the universe doesn't care whether a couple is homosexual, as long as there is love. How profound! It is fascinating to think the universe lays no judgement on the type of love, only the quality. How the Christian Right condemns homosexuality and all the pain that gay people experience because their families and colleagues cannot accept their sexual orientation is all so unwarranted. I have met numerous gay men who tried to deny their "gayness" by getting married to a woman, and all these marriages ended in agony. If the universe supports love, regardless of the form, and we all honored this openness, how much easier our lives would be.

Jasmine talked about a time on Earth when humans were more connected to the Creator and Earth Mother and the positive and negative energies were balanced. If this really was the case, I yearn for our planet to shift back to this. If there were ways that we could regain our sense of spirit and live more in our higher selves honoring the Creator and Earth Mother, then we need to learn them and quickly. With the current rates of environmental destruction and military aggression around the planet, we are very far from that balance presently.

When I first went to see Jasmine, I was in a very vulnerable, wounded place. I remember starting to leave a session early on feeling pained about life, and she pulled me to her side as she sat there. In the warmest, most nurturing voice, she said to me: "You know, Mare, God loves you." I will never forget that moment.

My father has tried to convey this to me many times, but I could never hear it the way he said it. This is probably because the God I thought he was talking about I had deemed to be a judgmental Catholic God. I had already walked away from that version of God. Whenever he would tell me, "You are loved," it seemed a part of his subtle attempts to pull me back into the Catholic church. And I, being the rebellious, strong-willed daughter that I am, had already decided that the Catholic God, wrapped up in the ethos that I needed to be forgiven for the sins that clouded my soul, was not a God that I choose to associate with. I choose a different God.

The God that Jasmine talked about is a powerful, loving God who accepts me totally and completely and fills my heart with warmth. There were no hoops of needing to be forgiven and muckraking through sins to keep me from being close to Him. The love from God that Jasmine talked about was so clean. God's clean, unconditional love.

To hear Jasmine say that God loves me and really take it in was one of the most powerful moments of my life. For if God loves me, then surely I am a good person, and there is much value to my life. Surely I can carry that love inside myself to give it back to Him and carry it into all that I do. This was a revelation beyond words. How I would like to carry that revelation to all whom I meet who suffer from a lack of love inside themselves. And I have met many people whom I so wanted to pull aside, as Jasmine pulled me aside, to tell them, "God so loves you, just as you are." But I censor myself for fear that they might be very uncomfortable with how clearly I see within them.

Yet God's love is there ~ for all of us to discover and connect with. Just as Earth Mother's love is there, too. All we need to do is reach out to Them.

✧

baltimore, maryland
january 2002

dear God...and Earth Mother...

    i woke up quite early this morning and could not coax myself back to sleep. this one new man in my life is on my mind. i have not scared Dan away so far and, considering how well we relate, he may be around for a long time to come. i can't believe i've finally found someone who may truly teach me the meaning of love here on Earth. i guess it's time.

and yesterday i was talking with my sister about what I've learned over the past six years of talking with people about God. her questions pushed me to realize that i never expected that i would find anyone who truly did have God's phone number. but i have ~ more than one person. in the process i've come to develop my own number. it's been amazing.

my sister confided that if she could call God, her big question to Him would be whether He absolutely loves her. i told her that only one other person asked that question in their interview, but my journey has brought me to that place of really knowing that You, God and Earth Mother, do love me ~ unconditionally. i deeply feel Your love continue to grow ~ the more i connect with You ~ and this has been the most incredible experience. i think my sister really heard me when i told her this. perhaps she can come to feel it too.

thank you, God/Creator and Earth Mother. thank you for all the teachers of my life ~ i'm glad to be here, glad to be doing what i am doing. my path has gotten stronger, with more clarity, more trust, more love than i have ever known.

i can't wait to see where You will lead me next.

i give You my humble love,
Your daughter,

mare

✦

We are living in a world that is absolutely transparent, and God is shining through it all the time. This is not just a fable or a nice story, it is true. And this is something we are not able to see. But if we abandon ourselves to Him and forget ourselves, we see it sometimes and we see it maybe frequently: that God manifests Himself everywhere, in everything ~ in people and in things and in nature and in events and so forth. So that it becomes very obvious that He is everywhere, He is in everything, and we cannot be without Him. You cannot be without God. It's impossible, it's simply impossible. The only thing is that we don't see it.

~ Thomas Merton

POSTSCRIPT

I was in the final stages of polishing up the punctuation on this manuscript and a friend sent this email to me. I think I might need to do my next book on God's address, so we all know where we could send this survey after we complete it! I'll keep you posted...

~ mare (holding her tongue in her cheek)

✧

Subject: Satisfaction Survey on God

God would like to thank you for your belief and patronage.

In order to better serve your needs, (S)He asks that you take a few moments to answer the following questions:

1. How did you find out about your deity?
__ Newspaper
__ Bible
__ Torah
__ Koran
__ Television
__ Book of Mormon
__ Divine Inspiration
__ Dead Sea Scrolls
__ My Mama Done Tol' Me

__ Near Death Experience
__ Near Life Experience
__ National Public Radio
__ Tabloid
__ Burning Shrubbery
__ The Receiving Course
__ Isaac MacSatsang
__ Other (specify): _____

2. Which model deity did you acquire?
__ Jehovah
__ Jesus
__ Krishna
__ Father, Son & Holy Ghost (Trinity Pak)
__ Zeus and entourage (Olympus Pak)
__ Odin and entourage (Valhalla Pak)
__ Allah
__ Satan
__ Gaia/Mother Earth/Mother Nature
__ God 1.0a (Hairy Thunderer)
__ God 1.0b (Cosmic Muffin)

3. Did your God come to you undamaged, with all parts in good working order and with no obvious breakage or missing attributes?
__ Yes
__ No

If no, please describe the problems you initially encountered here.
__ Not eternal
__ Finite in space/Does not occupy or inhabit the entire cosmos
__ Not omniscient
__ Not omnipotent
__ Not infinitely plastic (incapable of being all things to

all creations)
__ Permits sex outside of marriage
__ Prohibits sex outside of marriage
__ Makes mistakes
__ Makes or permits bad things to happen to good people
__ Makes or permits good things to happen to bad people
__ When beseeched, doesn't stay beseeched
__ Requires burnt offerings
__ Requires virgin sacrifices

4. What factors were relevant in your decision to acquire a deity? Please check all that apply.
__ Indoctrinated by parents
__ Needed a reason to live
__ Indoctrinated by society
__ Needed focus to despise
__ Needed focus to love
__ Imaginary friend grew up
__ Hate to think for myself
__ Wanted to meet girls/boys in church
__ Fear of death
__ Wanted to piss off parents
__ Wanted to please parents
__ Needed a day away from school or work
__ Desperate need for certainty
__ Like organ music
__ Need to feel morally superior
__ Thought Jerry Falwell was cool
__ Thought there had to be something other than Jerry Falwell
__ Shit was falling out of the sky
__ My shrubbery caught fire and told me to do it

5. Have you ever worshipped a deity before? If so, which

false god were you fooled by? Please check all that apply.
__ Baal
__ The Almighty Dollar
__ Left Wing Liberalism
__ The Radical Right
__ Amon Ra
__ Beelzebub
__ Bill Gates
__ Barney The Big Purple Dinosaur
__ The Great Spirit
__ The Great Pumpkin
__ The Sun
__ The Moon
__ The Force
__ Cindy Crawford
__ Elvis
__ A burning shrub
__ Psychiatry
__ Other: _____

6. Are you currently using any other source of inspiration in addition to God? Please check all that apply.
__ Tarot
__ Lottery
__ Astrology
__ Fortune cookies
__ Ann Landers
__ Psychic Friends Network
__ Dianetics
__ Palmistry
__ Playboy and/or Playgirl
__ Self-help books
__ Sex, drugs, and rock & roll
__ Biorhythms
__ Alcohol
__ Marijuana

__ Bill Clinton
__ Tea Leaves
__ EST
__ Amway
__ CompuServe
__ Mantras
__ Jimmy Swaggart
__ Crystals
__ Human sacrifice
__ Pyramids
__ Wandering around a desert
__ Insurance policies
__ Burning shrubbery
__ Barney T.B.P.D.
__ Barney Fife
__ Other:_____
__ None

7. God reputedly employs a limited degree of Divine intervention to preserve a balanced level of felt presence and blind faith. Which would you prefer?

Circle one below:

a. More Divine Intervention

b. Less Divine Intervention

c. Current level of Divine Intervention is just right

d. Don't know

e. What's Divine Intervention?

8. God also reputedly attempts to maintain a balanced level of disasters and miracles.

Please rate on a scale of 1 to 5 (1 = unsatisfactory, 5 = excellent) your opinion of the handling of the following:

a. Disasters:

1 2 3 4 5 flood

1 2 3 4 5 earthquake
1 2 3 4 5 war and holocausts
1 2 3 4 5 terrorism
1 2 3 4 5 pestilence
1 2 3 4 5 plague
1 2 3 4 5 spam
1 2 3 4 5 AOL

b. Miracles:
1 2 3 4 5 rescues
1 2 3 4 5 spontaneous remissions
1 2 3 4 5 stars hovering over tiny towns and previously
           unknown hamlets
1 2 3 4 5 crying statues
1 2 3 4 5 water changing to wine
1 2 3 4 5 walking on water
1 2 3 4 5 coincidence of any sort
1 2 3 4 5 getting any sex whatsoever

9. From time to time God reputedly makes available the names and addresses of Her/His followers and devotees to selected reputedly divine personages who provide quality services and perform intercessions in Her/His behalf. Are you interested in a compilation of listed offerings?

__ Yes, please deluge me with religious zealots for the benefit of my mortal soul
__ No, I do not wish to be inundated by religious fanatics clamoring for my money

10. Do you have any additional comments or suggestions for improving the quality of God's services? (Attach an additional sheet if necessary.)

(Circulating the World Wide Web)